DATE DUE

JUL 0 7			

THE
ORDINARY
WAY

THE ORDINARY WAY

A FAMILY SPIRITUALITY

Dolores R. Leckey

Crossroad · New York

1982

The Crossroad Publishing Company
575 Lexington Avenue, New York, NY 10022

Copyright © 1982 by Dolores R. Leckey

Printed in the United States of America

Library of Congress Cataloging in Publication Data

Leckey, Dolores R.
The ordinary way.

Includes index.
1. Family—Religious life. 2. Monastic and religious
life. 3. Spiritual life—Catholic authors. I. Title.
BX2351.L43   248.4   81–22206
ISBN 0–8245–0442–9   AACR2

Biblical quotations are taken from *The Jerusalem Bible* (copyright © 1966, 1967 and 1968 by Darton, Longman & Todd Ltd. and Doubleday & Company, Inc.) and the *Revised Standard Version of the Bible*, New Testament Section (first edition, copyright 1946; second edition © 1971 by Division of Christian Education of the National Council of the Churches of Christ in the United States of America).

For my husband, Tom
and for
Mary Kate, Tommy and Colum
Celia and Peter

CONTENTS

Foreword

It has often been said that, when Saint Benedict wrote his Rule for monks, he did not write a code book nor a set of job descriptions for an organization; rather, he wrote an analysis of a living organism based on the gospel of Jesus. Thus, the word *Rule* had a different meaning in the old days.

A monastery to Benedict was simply a Christian society based on the gospel. The abbot acted as a kind of "icon" of Christ, a perpetual reminder that the gathered community did not come together just for common work or mutual advantage, but structured itself on faith. From seeing Christ in the abbot, the monks were drawn to see Him in the guests, the sick, the old, the young—in everyone.

The daily round of prayer and work helped the monks keep the gospel and its values before their minds. There was nothing romantic about the whole routine, but life was "centered"—as we would say today—and the daily order assisted the monks in maintaining a Christian way of looking at the whole of life.

Most of all, the reminders in the Rule helped the monks learn how to base their relationships to God and among themselves on sincerity and truth. There could be no sham in the Rule. Standing so often before God each day, the monk was brought home to the realization of who he really was. His daily relationships to abbot and fellow-monks had to spring from that same sincerity. Any falseness would soon be detected.

Such a routine also resulted in a balance among many of life's tensions. Solitude and community demands, personal prayer and liturgy, interdependency and authority, work and leisure—all of these tugs and pulls in Christian life are dealt with in monasticism, but each person has to apply and re-apply daily the wisdom of the Rule to keep the personal equilibrium that is so easily thrown off course.

For all these reasons it is natural that spiritual writers have turned to the Rule of Benedict and the monastic tradition for the wisdom needed for the functioning of any family or society. Perhaps today, however, the monastic tradition has more to say to us than we at first imagined. It grew out of the extended family, but built a new kind of family relationship based on equality and love rather than on the Roman theory of paternal domination.

Dolores Leckey understands the essentials of the monastic tradition and the spiritual basis of the relationships within the Christian family. She is also a woman of our times. It is so refreshing to see someone like her reflect so profoundly on the family today in the light of the perennial wisdom of the ages that the monastic tradition encapsulated.

At the same time she shares her story so simply and frankly that one is immediately aware that she has personally understood well the monastic virtue of sincerity (Benedict would have called it humility).

Monks learned mostly from the example of other monks. The same is true today of all Christians, and we are, thus, grateful that Dolores Leckey has shared her personal journey that we might all learn.

Most Reverend Rembert G. Weakland, O.S.B.
Archbishop of Milwaukee

Acknowledgments

I am grateful for the opportunity to acknowledge publicly my debt to those who helped me, directly and indirectly, in the writing of this book. They include my friends and colleagues at the National Conference of Catholic Bishops and the Shalem Institute for Spiritual Formation: Rev. Tilden Edwards, director of Shalem, who counseled me in many ways; Rev. Daniel Hoye, General Secretary of the NCCB/USCC, who helped me find needed time and space in the midst of tight schedules and full calendars; Dr. Eugene Fisher, director of the Catholic-Jewish Secretariat of the NCCB, who shared with me his experience of writing a book while working full time; Ms. Patricia Davis, staff assistant to the Bishops' Committee on the Laity, who not only generously undertook more than her usual responsibilities in the Laity Secretariat during the weeks of writing but also read the manuscript with fine editorial expertise.

Others, too, gave graciously of their time and talent: Dr. Neal Vahle carefully and thoughtfully critiqued the manuscript. Rev. Aidan Shea, O.S.B., of Saint Anselm's Abbey in Washington, D.C., also offered editorial assistance. More importantly, our conversations over a period of time enlivened for me the Rule of Benedict, often in unexpected ways. Mrs. Joan Christenson typed the manuscript with great patience and care. Rev. Paul Wynants, C.I.C.M., provided me with solitude and hospitality at the Missionhurst Retreat Center in Arlington, Virginia, so that

I might have some uninterrupted writing time. I am grateful, too, to Msgr. Jan Schotte, C.I.C.M., who first introduced me to the Rule of Benedict, and to Richard Payne of The Crossroad Publishing Company for his steady direction and encouragement.

To all the men, women, and children, living and dead, who are part of *The Ordinary Way* my deepest appreciation. I hope I have been faithful to their unique revelations of God-with-us.

THE
ORDINARY
WAY

Introduction

The great ecclesial event of the twentieth century, the Second Vatican Council, issued a universal call to holiness, saying that all "of whatever rank or status are called to the fullness of Christian life."[1] For most of us this call is heard in families, with husband and wife, with children and with significant others. We hear the call in their presence, day after day, in the complexity and fragility of our particular environments. This pattern of family life is what I have called the ordinary way.

The families I know and who are part of this book follow the ordinary way of holiness along many different paths. Many are two-parent families, but how they live out their vocations as husband and wife, mother and father, form different stories. Some of these families could be called traditional insofar as the husband is the principal financial support of the family and the wife is the principal caretaker of the house and children. In some cases both parents work outside the home and that experience is leading to new experiments in shared responsibility for domestic life. I know a few families where the husband and father is the at-home parent, principally engaged with children, household tasks, and neighborhood duties, while the wife and mother works outside the home and provides the necessary financial resources.

Also reflected in these pages are families where death or divorce has altered the basic structure of the family and one adult now bears alone the responsibility for the rearing of the children. There is also the phenomenon of the single parent, never married, who reflects a unique dimension of family and faith.

Alternative families, that is, people who have chosen to live in extended Christian households, are also here. These households may consist of single adults, married couples, and families with children; some include a priest in the household.

It is clear to me, therefore, that to speak with any degree of authenticity about Christian families in today's world, one must be aware of the range of possibilities for forming families, and the variety of household communities that call themselves "family."

The changing shape of family life is often interpreted by social scientists as an attack on the family as an institution. Their assessment frequently finds agreement from pastors and other church ministers who deal with parish and family life on a regular basis. What do they really mean? Do they mean that ours is the first generation of families to feel stress? This is certainly not the case. The golden age of the family is more myth than reality. In truth, every generation of families has had to live with challenges and difficulties. Most of our ancestors lived with the constant threat of plagues and persecutions. Until fairly recent times death and disease frequently separated children from their parents; orphanages were a much more prominent feature of our landscape than they are today. Many of us include in our history men and women who faced the relentless hardships of pioneer life or immigration, as our great-grandparents or grandparents or even parents searched for a stable and safe place to live and work. Furthermore, until this century, women and children lived a precarious existence, without the protection of law. Stress is not new to family life.

What is new, I suggest, is the origin of stress. The strain that late-twentieth-century families feel is more internal than external. We are faced not with armed attack in the woods or exile or death from epidemics so much as an attack of confidence in our worth as persons, in our strength and purpose as family.

We live in an age and in a culture that values planning and evaluation, production and achievement. Families can and do feel the stress of expectations because, unlike other social units, they do not measure output. They do not fit the technological criteria for success because their content is personal interrelatedness with all the inherent unpredictability and ambiguity of human behavior. Family equations cannot be solved with computer precision because at the heart of the family, I believe, there dwells the unsolvable mystery, the One who cannot be contained or measured. In this way family life seems at odds with the rest of society, and rightly so. Therein lies the prophetic potential of the family.

It is important to remember that no matter how unusual a family's shape may be, grace is there, in all the odd spaces and details that make up *that* family's life. This is poignantly illustrated in *Housekeeping*, a novel by Marilynne Robinson. The narrator of the story is Ruthie, an adolescent whose parents and grandmother have died, leaving her and her sister, Lucille, on their own. Their Aunt Sylvie, a type of shopping-bag lady, has come to the family home and has been caring for the girls in her own peculiar way. The home has come to resemble a train station under Sylvie's casual approach to housekeeping. Lucille, unable to relate to this transient approach to life and ashamed of her aunt's strange ways, has taken up residence with a sympathetic schoolteacher. Ruthie, who resembles Sylvie in temperament, remains. Some townswomen, worried about Ruthie's future, come to visit this now reduced family, to persuade Sylvie that Ruthie, too, should find a new home. Speaking about Ruthie, one of the women says:

> "She looks so sad."
> And Sylvie replied, "Well, she *is* sad."
> Silence.

Sylvie said, "She should be sad." She laughed.

"I don't mean she *should* be, but, you know, who wouldn't be?"

Again, silence.

"That's how it is with family," Sylvie said. "You feel them the most when they're gone. I knew a woman once who had four children, and she didn't seem to care for them at all. She'd give them string beans for breakfast, and she never even cared if their shoes matched. That's what people told me. But I knew her when she was old, and she had nine little beds in her house, all made up, and every night she'd go from one to another, tucking the children in, over and over again. She just had four, but after they were all gone she had nine. Well, she was probably crazy.

But you know what I mean . . ."

Silence.

"Now I look at Ruthie and I see Helen [Ruthie's mother], too. That's why families are so important. Other people walk out the door and they're gone."

Silence. A shifting of the couch . . .

"Families should stay together. Otherwise things get out of control. My father, you know. I can't even remember what he was like, I mean when he was alive. But ever since, it's Papa here and Papa there, and dreams . . . Like the poor woman with nine children. She was walking the floor the whole night." . . . "Families should stay together," Sylvie said. "They should. There is no other help. Ruthie and I have trouble enough with the ones we've lost already."[2]

One of the assumptions behind *The Ordinary Way* is that God and grace are indeed present in all kinds of families, in those with compatible spouses, orderly children, and neat dinner tables, and in those we might call marginal, the Sylvies and Ruthies. Sylvie loves, and so grace abounds—even in her neuroses. I think that Sylvia and Ruthie and the townspeople sensed that graced Mystery, even if they didn't directly say so, or couldn't name it theologically. And so it is for most of us. The call to holiness and community that happens in our unique and imperfect families may be unnamed. It can be obscured or forgotten or lost in the endless cares of commuter traffic, illness, dinner parties, report cards, gardens, home maintenance, relationships, committees, newspapers, not to mention sin. And yet, Christian spirituality and community are irrevocably intertwined. If we are to grow into the fullness of Christ, it will be in the context of community.

Both the secular society and the church society are concerned about families and are attempting to respond to what are perceived to be family needs. Churches of various denominations, alarmed at the rising divorce rate, are paying more attention to marriage preparation and marriage enrichment. Family counseling is increasingly available to all, regardless of income. In all of these expressions of concern, however, family ministry often takes the form of yet another program or another technique or another plan for making better families. Underlying this approach is the belief that families really ought to look elsewhere for their strength and meaning. There is a hint that something is fundamentally wrong with people and families, and ministry should "fix it up." Pope Paul VI challenged this view when he called the family "the domestic Church."[3] This is a profound statement coming as it does after Vatican II, which described the Church as a pilgrim people, not yet perfected, but in need of continual renewal and reform. This insight about families being a microcosm of church was reiterated during the 1980 Synod on the Family when the bishops acknowledged that the family was not so much the object of evangelization, to be converted by "the real Church," as the agent of evangelization, with members ministering to each other and to the world. What this says is that the family contains within it the drama of ongoing death and resurrection that is the essence of Christian spirituality.

Since the Second Vatican Council, many lay movements specifically concerned with spiritual life and growth in families have appeared. The contribution of these movements to the overall strengthening of couples and families, and of the Church, cannot be denied. There is a temptation, however, to mistake technique and programs for conversion and transformation. There is also an ever-present temptation to assume that somewhere there is exactly the right model for marriage or for family spirituality. In searching for the right model, we can miss the grace that is always with us. The very nature of spirituality, its source and dynamic quality, precludes the fixing of spiritual standards. At the same time families do need some ways of understanding how their shared life can bring them to a deeper awareness of their being and living in God. Caught between a culture that generates chaos and confusion on the one hand, and the rigidity of fundamentalist religion on the other, families who want to practice a Christian humanism need some kind of structure, one that is tested and strong and yet elastic. Such a structure is part of the Catholic Christian tradition.

From the beginnings of Christian history, when serious seekers moved to the desert to find union with God, a model or paradigm for being together has been available for Christian communities of all kinds. It is monasticism. Discussions about the need for models of lay spirituality for our time tend to reject automatically anything containing the word monastic. This facile dismissal may come from priests who know little about adult responsibility in the family, or from laypeople who have been given a stereotyped view of monasticism and who sometimes report what they have heard from non-monks. And yet, as I continue on the Christian journey, reflecting on my own experience and hearing the stories of others who are continually engaged in seeking the face of God in the web of our lay existence, certain qualities of life and certain dynamics commonly valued in the spiritual quest emerge and are named. In the naming I have recognized the dimensions of Christian community that we call monasticism. Saint Benedict's vision of the households of God has great meaning, I suggest, for family life in these last years of the twentieth century.

Every age has brought its own form of enculturation to bear on the monastic model. The farther human experience is removed from a form, the emptier the form becomes for people. Reactions against monasticism as an appropriate teacher of spirituality for our time are often reactions against outdated formalism and rigid institutionalism. When we peel off the layers of cultural accretion, however, what do we find? Not so much a treatise on spirituality or a strict regimen, but rather more a way of simply being in life, of setting up a household— Benedict's household of God.

The original vision of Benedict's monastic way was decidedly domestic, and laymen of all ages, from youngsters to elders, formed the household. There they sought God, not by unusual or esoteric means, but in the ordinary events and rhythms of daily life. One purpose of this book is to draw forth and name those characteristics of community life that centuries of experience affirm as helpful guideposts on the spiritual journey. Another is to name them in such a way as to make sense in our culture, for our time, within the varieties of ordinary families.

Since Benedict's monastic households were—and are—same-sex families, one might question the appropriateness of relating this model to families where the sexes are usually mixed. My response is that the conversation between theology and the social sciences increasingly points toward the fact of *personhood* as the fundamental human reality. The implication of this for reflections on family life is that families are communities of persons, as are monasteries.

The patterns of communal life flowing from Benedict's vision are patterns of life and holiness based on the ordinary dynamics of personality and of human need and desire. How we might apply them to families of men and women and children, bound together in different ways and with different styles and tastes in a rapidly changing culture, is the central focus of this book.

Not all of the observances contained in the Rule of Benedict apply to contemporary Christian family life. Indeed, not all apply to contemporary monasteries. But there are certain elements of monastic structure that are readily applicable to families. I have identified nine, each the subject of a chapter in which I look at the element or dynamic as it is traditionally expressed in monasticism and then reflect on how I see it lived in today's families. I begin with *intimacy,* which has been called the pivotal factor in married spirituality.[4] The second chapter concerns *equality,* particularly the equality between men and women in both the domestic and professional worlds. I do not treat manual labor—work—which was (and is) prominent in the Rule of Benedict as a separate chapter, but it is present in the practical discussion of equality. *Authority* is the topic of chapter 3. I approach authority from the perspective of shared responsibility for the conduct of the family community and relate it to the giftedness of the family members and to the developmental stages of life. Chapter 4 explores *prayer,* alone and in common, and assumes its centrality in the life of an intentionally Christian family; this is followed by a chapter on *solitude* and *silence,* which, I argue, are necessary for a sane and ordered family life. Chapter 6 takes note of the importance of *play* in the development of a contemplative life-style (although this is not found in Benedict's Rule), while chapter 7, on *study,* looks at the ways creativity and continuing education of all kinds can be enhanced by family commitments. *Stability* is the subject of chapter 8, admittedly one of the foundations of family life, but also subject to the subtleties of interpretation. The final chapter is a reflection on *hospitality,* and it attempts to integrate the other dynamics into the community rhythm of receiving and reaching out to others to forge the bonds of human and Christian solidarity. Intimacy, equality, authority, prayer, solitude, play, study, stability, and hospitality are the elements of intentional Christian communities, which I see as doorways to God in ordinary family life.

While the organization of this book tends to present these monastic elements as discrete and separate, in actuality they weave in and out of each other and together bring a wholeness and balance to common life, whether in a monastery or in a family.

As I worked on the different chapters, I found that some came easily, the experience readily available to share. Others were more difficult for me to write. I think this reflects the reality that we all experience. Some of these ways of being with and in God are natural to us. They are our strengths. We feel at home with them. Others test us more, stretch us, make us a bit uncomfortable. But I believe that a full life, rich in the possibilities of God, requires some attention to the undeveloped sides of our individual and corporate lives.

In writing *The Ordinary Way* I have been influenced by many disciplines, including psychology, theology and Scripture, the social sciences and literature, and the growing body of spiritual writings. The most important influence, though, is experience —what I have come to know by reflecting on *my* story as it continues to unfold within the boundaries of my particular family, and on the stories of others who continue to share life generously with me. They are real people, those who appear in this book. In one or two instances a name has been changed or left out for the sake of confidentiality. In all cases it has been their storytelling that has made the writing of this book something of a pilgrimage for me.

Chapter 1

INTIMACY

Thy face, Lord, do I seek
Hide not thy face from me
Psalm 27

The first question addressed to our ancestors was, "Where are you?" The questioner is God, moving through the garden of Genesis, seeking and asking a question that has echoed through all the gardens of human history. And Adam speaks for all of us when he admits his fear of being seen naked. He does what is human. He hides from God. But God is not deterred. God seeks and finds and sees.

Our scriptural heritage is filled with expressions of longing and searching for God, sometimes expressed as God's seeking after us, as in the garden narrative. The revelation of self and the revelation of God are different sides of the same reality. Both revelations are costly, however, involving great personal risk. When Moses, for example, stands before the burning bush —a revelation of God and of Moses' deepest self—the experience proves too much for him. Afraid, he covers his face. Later, during the divine encounter on Mount Sinai, God tells Moses, "Warn the people not to pass beyond their bounds to come and look on Yahweh, or many of them will lose their lives" (Ex. 19:21).

During all the years of desert wandering, Yahweh seems to prefer hiddenness. The "cloud of divine presence" lingers close by the people, but it is never open or even transparent. Nor do the people seem to want a more intimate relationship at this point in religious development.

On the other hand, the Psalms explicitly express the desire for deep union with God. They also illustrate that God's presence is not so elusive after all. In fact, the Psalms contain a vast range of possibilities for meeting God. The divine presence is in rivers and mountains, in fire and ice, in music and in darkness. The presence is as much in poverty and emptiness as in the rich and overflowing events of life. A rhythm of closeness and withdrawal pervades these Scriptures. God is sometimes experienced as present, sometimes as absent, and it is both rhythms which give form to the human-divine relationship.

This oscillation is most evident in the Song of Songs. Here, the beloved calls and beckons, "Come . . . my love . . . winter is past, the rains are over and gone, the flowers appear on the earth." "Show me your face," he pleads. But when the bride, "trembling to the core of her being," rises to open the door to her beloved, "he had turned his back and gone" (Fourth Poem). There is no sense of despair, however, The seeking is felt to be as important as the final encounter and is itself an act of deepest intimacy.

The definitive insertion of God into human history in the person of Jesus makes it clear that the human-divine relationship is also costly to God, costly unto death. It also makes clearer *how* we are to seek the face of God; we are to seek—and find—the God of Moses, of the Psalms, the God of Jesus in each other. In varied ways Jesus says: Turn to one another; God is there. His growing intimacy with Martha and Mary and Lazarus, his encounters with Nicodemus and the Samaritan woman—and others—all become the means of revealing the divine within the human community. When Jesus talks with his friends, it is often about losing their lives. Undoubtedly, there are many levels of meaning here. Certainly one way of understanding this saying is that when we allow others to see us as we are, and when we see others as they are, we recognize the root of our common existence. What dies is the false sense of separate lives. Sometimes this realization is too much to bear all at once, and, like Moses, we must cover our faces. But there is more. Jesus takes the heart of the Old Testament law and presents it to us, free of accretions. "The Lord God is One. You must love the Lord your God with all your heart, with all your soul, with all your mind, with all your strength," and you do this, he explains, by loving your neighbor. This neighbor may be very close by, or a stranger yet unseen.

The kind of community life that Jesus shares with others is filled with the details of intimacy. The itinerant nature of his ministry lends itself to personal revelation. We have all experienced a journey as a special kind of environment, where self-disclosure seems safe and where there is a willingness to receive another person's confidences. Travelers often find themselves in a confessional atmosphere, sharing life stories with strangers. This is typical of a pilgrimage event, a sign of the interdependence of those journeying together.

Jesus' meetings with others along the way are almost always characterized by signs of intimacy. His eating and drinking with others is important enough to be noted in several Gospel accounts. He gives time and energy to conversation, to what Martin Buber calls dialogue. Over and over one is struck by his art of being present, and how this presence acts as a mirror of revelation in the other. One senses, for example, the amazement of the woman at the well as she realizes that she is being seen and known so thoroughly. But she is not threatened by this. Rather, she is strengthened. Perhaps she feels this knowledge and power are grounded in love and compassion rather than judgment. Perhaps she sees herself reflected in Jesus' eyes and knows that she is loved.[1]

Intimacy was a distinguishing mark of the early Christian communities. The Acts of the Apostles is as much a story of Christians belonging to one another as it is of early missionary adventures. The sharing of common life and goods is a predominant theme: "The faithful all lived together and owned everything in common" (Acts 2:44–45).

Even the desert way of early Christian life was marked by intimacy. Men and women who sought spiritual direction from the desert fathers and mothers would simply come and live with the spiritual guide, watching his or her way of life, asking questions, revealing secret thoughts and feelings, fears and desires. The spiritual guide would discern what was of God and what was not. In this intimate exchange, then, one grew in the knowledge and love of God. Monastic communities, patterned along domestic lines, assumed a certain intimate quality. However, the earliest monastic authors hesitated to affirm the value of particular intimate friendships, for a number of reasons. There was concern about factions forming around personalities; there was also concern about the danger of sexual temptation. Therefore, the experience of the love of God in and for another was rarely touched upon in the early writings.

Later in the course of monasticism (eleventh and twelfth centuries), Saint Anselm, Saint Bernard, and William of St.-Thierry all wrote vividly of communion with persons. But it was Saint Aelred of Rievaulx who brought clarity to the vision of friendship as a path to God within the context of community living. He unhesitatingly admitted the dangers of false friendships, but clearly maintained that the advantages of true intimacy for the spiritual person outweighed these dangers.

Aelred's classic, *Spiritual Friendship,* has had many different applications through the centuries. Of particular interest for these reflections on family life is the interpretation of Kenneth Russell, who sees many parallels between monastic spiritual friendship and marital intimacy.[2] He observes that in marriage a couple can evolve together in a friendship that grows more and more intense; as in Aelred's model, each spouse will *not* seek personal advantage, but will delight in the good of the other. It will be a path of mutual equality and intimacy as the spouses move trustingly toward God.

We have just come through a period of all kinds of human potential groups that some have classified as easy intimacy. These groups have sometimes demonstrated that even in marriage and family life intimacy may be absent. On the other hand, they have occasionally helped husbands, wives, parents, and friends to be more aware of each other and more fully present to all persons. More significant, perhaps, than the successes and failures is the underlying awareness that there still remains that longing to look upon the face of God. The same thrust toward *communio*, that is, the existentially realized unity of persons which characterized the early Church, the pilgrimages of the Middle Ages, and the monastic way of life, is still part of the human search. In our time it is possible to realize the intimacy of *communio* in family life through the several kinds of relationships found there: between husband and wife, parent and child, and in friendship with others outside the immediate family circle.

Husband-Wife

The intimacy of marriage is unique.

First, there is the publicly expressed intent to remain in intimate relationship with each other, forever. Before a gathered community of the Church, a Christian man and a woman declare;

> I take you to be my wife/husband.
> I promise to be true to you in good times and in bad,
> in sickness and in health. I will love you and honor
> you all the days of my life.

This public statement of intent reflects the values of reliability and predictability that create a climate of safety so that one can risk being known by the other, and not rejected.

During the course of the years, however, various factors can and do intervene. The climate of trust may erode; separation and divorce may occur. When this happens, one is at a crossroad in the spiritual life. A new route must be found and traveled in faith. This is difficult if not impossible without the support and companionship of the Christian community. Separation is one of the realities not only of married life, but of community life of all kinds and, indeed, of *all life.* This does not mean, however, that a man and a woman entering a sacramental marriage do not normally intend and expect an enduring intimacy with each other. They do. And in this intention they reflect a kind of love that for Christians is supreme and ultimate.

Second, the way of ongoing intimacy in marriage is specifically sexual, and this is different from other close relationships. Sexual intercourse is not the only expression of an intimate shared life in marriage, but it is centrally located in the relationship. Sexual presence is one of the primary ways we unmask. We know and are known as we are: body, mind, spirit, emotions. One's whole being is engaged. Ann Ulanov states that in a committed and loving sexual relationship we work directly on being.

> We are opened and seen in a total way comparable only to our earliest relation with a loving mother, or to a profound religious experience. We are exposed for what we are with foibles, faults, possibilities, talents, beauties, imperfections—in the flesh, without disguise or hiding. We are inspected. Mirrored back in the face of the lover, we discover our true image.[3]

She further explains that the depth of this encounter accounts for the devastating effects of a failed love affair or marriage. One feels abused at the very core of one's being.

When not abused, however, the sexual bond can demonstrate an intensive being for one's neighbor, and can summon one from ego-centeredness to attentiveness to the other. Pope John Paul II observed that husbands and wives "grow as persons

. . . mutually, and one for the other, through their bodies, . . . this also incorporates psychological and spiritual intimacy and creates deep bonding."[4]

Although marital sexuality is only one expression of intimacy and can be empty and automatic without a fuller context of shared life, it remains a principal way of ministering to each other in marriage, a way of establishing and maintaining connectedness. All members of the family are affected by the expression of sexual love between wife and husband. Sexual love seems to be an especially valuable means of bridging the inevitable estrangements that happen because of illness or travel or other life obligations that can remove one from the intimate rhythms of life.

In a recent novel, *Dale Loves Sophie to Death,* the principal characters, Dinah and her husband, Martin, are apart over the course of a summer. Dinah, with their three children, visits the small town in which she grew up. Martin remains at home in the New England college town where he is teaching summer classes. At the end of the summer they are reunited, and they begin to build bridges to each other through the ordinary act of marital sex.

> But later, when they finally settled themselves in the same bed, they were both made easier by their instinctive inclination to turn toward the other. Each one had expected that the other would be too tired to make love. In fact, they made love with a gentle and slow pleasure, because their energy was not great. Their passion was not ragged or insistent, and Dinah was glad that her body was allowing her this great enjoyment; she wasn't hindered by vanity and self-evaluation; she was not being judged. The two of them were always reliable, so that they lay in bed after making love, satisfied and no longer needful in any way, for the time being. Dinah was thinking that sex can be the sweetest, kindest way to overcome reticence. They both felt at ease at last, and

in the morning they were fond and affectionate with each other and with the children. Their physical isolation from the other had made them forget how to be familiar, and now they remembered.[5]

This passage describes the mutual ordinary ministry that is constitutive of marriage. It is interesting, however, to see how all the sacraments are marked by physical interraction. In the sacrament of reconciliation, for example, the Christian reveals the secrets of the soul, with all its meanness and self-serving behaviors, to the priest or pastor, who in turn speaks words of understanding and forgiveness. Sometimes the penitent is physically touched, i.e., with a laying on of hands, the ancient sign of the gift of the Spirit. Words and touch, then, mark God's presence in this sacrament. In the sacrament of the eucharist we are offered consecrated bread and wine to eat and drink, an act of spiritual nourishment. In marriage, sexual intercourse is the primary (though certainly not the only) ritual of the sacrament. It is an extension and fulfillment of the partners' ministry to each other begun during the public statement of vows. Sexual intimacy is also a way of discovering how we relate to God. Are we guarded, self-seeking, manipulative, accepting, surrendering, fearful, trusting, willful, respectful? Are we seeking mutuality with its implicit co-responsibility? Or are we opting for dependence rather than interdependence?

The intimacy of marriage, like that of all Christian communities, implies an openness to being influenced by the other as well as to exercise influence. As one's capacity for change and growth is enlarged, one's idea and experience of God is expanded. No one who is committed to love is exempt from the possibility of change, not even Jesus. The Gospel story of the Greek woman (as related in Mark) who begs Jesus to rid her daughter of demons is such an illustration. At first, Jesus refuses her request, saying his ministry is first to his own people, the Jews. He is even insulting in his refusal: "It is not right to take the children's bread and throw it to the dogs." The woman's love for her daughter compels her to respond deeply and honestly to Jesus, and she replies that even the dogs under the table eat the children's crumbs. In this encounter, Jesus' concept of his mission seems at first narrow. His human identity is attached to his mission to the Jews, but not so attached that he cannot be affected by love. He changes his mind and cures her daughter.

Openness in the exchange of love becomes a movement toward human solidarity. This movement does not happen at a steady, rapid pace. According to recent research, marital intimacy, including sexual expression and emotional closeness, appears to be cyclical. The cycle includes falling in love, settling into a routine, descending into a crisis, and beginning again. The cycle repeats itself often in marriage, with varying degrees of intensity, depending on the circumstances.[6] Archbishop Bernardin called attention to this phenomenon in a position paper presented at the 1980 World Synod of Bishops in Rome, likening it to the paschal mystery.

> An initially unconscious evil in married life and one which emerges gradually, imperceptibly at first, is that increasing indifference of spouses toward each other which arises from their need for autonomy and freedom. It becomes conscious sin when, knowing their mutual feelings of disappointment and hurt, they deliberately withhold communication. This sin becomes murderous hatred, a virtual crucifixion of the self and the other, when at last an explosion occurs in which torrents of vicious recriminations are loosed. Yet it is precisely here, at the painful heart of the mystery and almost simultaneously with accusations intended to wound and destroy, that the possibility exists for sorrow, born of acknowledgement of sin, to call forth forgiveness—a forgiveness so deep and purifying that the relationship is truly born anew. . . . Evil becomes sin, sin becomes murderous hatred, murderous hatred gives

way to sorrow, and out of sorrow is born forgiveness—
or resurrection—all because the co-victims on the
cross, the self and the spouse, are loved. For persons
who have this experience, the Christ they crucify is not
out there, beyond their deepest feelings. Rather this
Christ is as close as their own hearts. Indeed, it is their
very heart, the love of their life, enfleshed in their
beloved, toward whom their sorrow in the face of truth
and their forgiveness in the face of love are felt and
savored, thereby generating powerful creative forces,
resurrection.[7]

People who have been married for many years sometimes
speak of the depth of intimacy felt by being quiet together,
simply being in the same room or the same house, conscious of
each other's presence. There may be little or no conversation
or direct interaction of any kind, but there is a feeling of nearness that comes from a reservoir of shared experience. It builds
up bit by bit over the years to an intense awareness of the other.

Persons of prayer will recognize similarities in the cycles of
marital intimacy and the cycles of the spiritual life. Periods of
dryness in prayer, indifference, fatigue, inner turmoil, as well as
delight and consolation are well-known on the spiritual journey.
Through experience and reflection, though, we come to know
God in the periods of absence as well as presence. In marriage,
as in prayer, sometimes the appropriate response is simply to
wait.

The Practice of Intimacy

The original rupture in Genesis between man and woman has
had many effects. Some of these will be discussed in the chapter
on equality. One effect has been the tendency of both men and
women to prefer independence rather than intimacy. The ever-
present temptation is for independent action over and against
shared life.

Because intimacy leads to change, often quite painful change, the habit of resistance develops early. Other habits—promptness, tact, neatness, and so on—can be developed through patience and attention. So can marital intimacy. Beyond the day-to-day sharing of food, shelter, children, friends, resources, we need to decide that we will be present to each other, in some intentional way, on some regular basis. Some marriage and family-life movements promote methods within marriage to facilitate this. For example, the Teams of Our Lady, an international movement dedicated to enriching marital spirituality, require a monthly talk session between husband and wife. This is not to be a problem-solving session so much as a faith-and-heart talk. Marriage Encounter promotes a daily dialogue, written and verbal, wherein the spouses share their feelings with each other. Spiritual direction or pastoral counseling often suggest ways of incorporating the practice of marital intimacy into one's own rule of life. This may range from regular periods of shared Scripture and prayer to attentively caring for the body.

Parent-Child

All Christian community is basically about being human. The gentle practice of intimacy in marriage is one of the most ordinary ways of realizing this, but certainly not the only way. Within the family structure, the parent-child relationship is also one of natural intimacy. It is a bond that is frequently used to describe God's relationship with the human race. In the Old Testament, God is spoken of as father and mother, as a powerful creator, and as one who gives birth, nurtures, and protects the offspring.[8] To Jesus, God was Abba, a term unusual in Jewish prayer at that time because of its childlike, uninhibited familiarity. In his teaching about God, Jesus likened God to a father who has unconditional love for his children.

My first child was born twenty-three years ago. I still remember a great deal about the pregnancy and delivery. Present to me in an especially vivid way are those moments immediately after the birth of my daughter. These moments were flooded with a sense of our closeness. She had lived and grown in my own body and she had emerged a perfect little being, beautiful beyond all telling. My feeling of closeness to her was balanced, however, by a knowledge that in this newly born person a life was underway over which neither I nor my husband would have any ultimate control. She had a future, the shape of which I only partially knew. She was free. She would enter into relationships, affect other persons, choose a vocation, perhaps some day herself give birth. At that moment of intense intimacy between us, I also saw the infinite distance. Yet I somehow knew that God was in both the closeness and the distance.

My children were born before the use of birthing rooms and the father's participation in the delivery. I am told that today many fathers who assist in the birth of their children also feel this deep sense of bonding.

That parents influence infants and young children in the furthest recesses of their beings is well documented. Little has been said, however, about the young child's influence on parents, especially on their spiritual growth and development. In our time, the transition to parenthood is probably the decisive movement toward adulthood. It is the time when we assume full responsibility for the life and well-being of another person. This has the potential for pulling us toward transcendence, not all at once, but over a period of time.

Bernard Lonergan's transcendental imperatives—"be attentive, be intelligent, be reasonable, be responsible, develop and if necessary, change"—are remarkably applicable to parenthood.[9] They are also remarkably applicable to the development of contemplative prayer. For what is contemplation but paying absolute attention to the hidden God, coming ever more fully under the divine influence, recognizing the true relatedness of all life, and the needs of others as our own needs? Who is the contemplative but one who comes to greater and greater consciousness of living and moving and having all being in

Christ? Is it not seeing more clearly, with less distortion, and finally understanding even as we have been understood? (1 Cor. 13:12)

Children help this process of seeing and understanding. In them we see ourselves reflected, not only the obvious characteristics of physique and style and mannerisms, but also repressed parts of ourselves. To become the loving bearers of tradition that our children need us to be, those shadow sides of our personality must be allowed to surface; and then they must be owned. Spiritual growth is precisely this: bringing to light that which was formerly hidden, acknowledging who we really are, confessing and repenting, if needed, and being grateful always.[10]

Contemplation is also delight, enjoying God and knowing that God enjoys us. The moments when, as parents (or as teachers) we stop judging our children, and are simply *with* them in the joy of discovery, are moments of simple, natural contemplation. We have become, for a short while at least, like little children.

As the contemplative capacity increases, one is drawn into a process of letting go. Sometimes a total letting go is demanded. So it was with Nancy, the mother of three sons. Her firstborn son was retarded and suffered also from muscular dystrophy. His condition required institutionalization, and eventually he died. When John, Nancy's second son, was also diagnosed as having muscular dystrophy, it seemed at first like a cruel joke. But John was bright, and had a strong sense of self. He attended school almost until the end. John's interests extended far beyond wheelchairs and clinics. According to friends, he was an expert on baseball and could draw intricate maps of all kinds of places, real and imaginary.

Everyone who knows the family describes the relationship between Nancy and John as normal—John could be trying, as any teenage boy, and Nancy could get angry—yet unusually close. Eventually all John's physical care depended on his mother, with some help from a younger brother. It was a special kind of intimacy that can best be termed communion. Together they learned about living and dying. Church was important to John. He sensed his part in the whole body. His life had many limitations, but he could pray, and he did. People came to him, in fact, and asked for his prayers. He accepted their requests in the same way another boy would accept being asked to rake the leaves.

Nancy, always aware that John would not live to adulthood, decided to *live* that particular experience rather than deny it. She wrote poetry as a way of letting go of John, whose life had become as close to her as her own. One of her poems follows:

MEDITATION ON WATCHING

"Could you not watch one hour with Me."

"You have to watch him carefully," said a friend, speaking of my son.
Yes, I surely do—Especially when the litany begins—

1:00 A.M. "Mom, my ankle hurts, please come in."

2:30 A.M. "Mom, move my ankle."

4:30 A.M. "Ma, my ankle hurts, come in."

At this point, Mom only wishes for sleep—
But sleep doesn't come for her either.
The instinct to ignore the plaintive voice is there—
But for the tired realization—which grows stronger
in such moments, that, "well, suppose Jesus was calling—
(He is, of course, and the reality is so clear), wouldn't
you help him?" Think of His ankles on the Cross (sudden
thought—tell this slowly fading child to think of Jesus
and how His ankle bones hurt so bad at Calvary.)

The litany of calling ends for this night; but this has been
a month of such litanies—a busy month—so push the

thoughts back—push the unspoken insights back.
Yet the reminder is there; "You have to watch him
carefully."
And at such moments the reality breaks through
Dying takes a lifetime—and this dying will take two
lifetimes—
Yours and the child's. But his dying, like all men's, will
be his alone and uniquely. You are only the watcher, the
occasional comforter (never knowing if your words help);
knowing only that watch you must and comfort you must.

The litany continues for another night, sometimes skipping
a night or two. Brace by day—"Pull it up, Mom"; "Pull it
down, please"; "It's too tight"—and now a sore ankle by
night.
One is encompassed by God's presence so strong in His
Spirit
in one, small, thin pain-wracked body. Sleep-bereft mother—
longing for rest, yet dimly aware of His sustaining care in
every call of: "Mom, my ankle hurts." The lived reality so
much more powerful than imagined ones. Powerful in the
sense
that all suffering enlarges one's heart.[11]

Not many of us learn these lessons so vividly. But there are
other ways of dying in the parent-child relationship, little ways
woven into the ordinary experience of all of us. As children
move toward the critical adolescent years, filled with varying
degrees of ambivalence for everybody, parents are newly challenged to be faithful to the God-like task of freeing their children. The former patterns of intimacy between parent and child
are reshaped. Rather than continual emotional and physical
involvement with their children, parental love takes the form of
background. Like God, we are more a presence than active
agents, enabling our children to exercise autonomy and responsibility. Growing children know this loving presence is firmly

rooted in their lives, but hidden like roots, allowing the new foliage to grace the world in its own way.

One father I know told his fourteen-year-old son, "You may run away from us in your mind and in your imagination, but we will be here when you want to return. We are your community. We will care for your wounds and help you reconcile the mistakes you are bound to make."

To trust the growing autonomy of the teenage child, *really* to trust, is to trust in ever more radical ways the action of God in the family community. One day I asked myself: If I believed God's grace was motivating my life, why did I doubt that grace was also operative in my teenage children? The question has been reformulated many times, in many ways, through the years. Each time the response has required a little less clinging and grasping on my part, and a fuller admission that *God is God.*

Friendship

"Friendship is a stage bordering upon that perfection which consists in the love and knowledge of God, so that man from being a friend of his fellowman becomes the friend of God, according to the words of the Savior in the Gospel: 'I will not now call you servants, but my friends.' " This is the observation of Aelred of Rievaulx, a twelfth-century monk, in his treatise *Spiritual Friendship.* Using the genre of the dialogue, Aelred elaborates on the characteristics and value of genuine friendship, distinguishing between the advantages that flow from friendship and the love inherent in the friendship. He says: "Your friend is the companion of your soul, to whose spirit you join and attach yours, and so associate yourself that you wish to become one instead of two, since he is one to whom you entrust yourself as to another self, from whom you hide nothing, from whom you fear nothing."[12]

Aelred is echoing Jesus when he makes the explicit connection between friendship, love, and unity. When Jesus speaks of love he does so in terms of giving of one's life. On the night before his death he demonstrates what he means by love and friendship in the eloquently tender act of washing his friends' feet. He then turns to God and speaks about the unity that exists between them, and prays that his friends will also know this unity. Rich as it is in symbol and summons to friendship, this final evening of Jesus' life on earth is also a synthesis of many days and nights of ordinary interaction that form and stabilize friendships everywhere. Jesus had spent time with his friends—wasted time, some might say—eating, drinking, talking, listening to them. This evening recalled so many other evenings when they shared their dreams and hopes for the future, and other times when Jesus concentrated the force of his personality to mend the broken lives that touched his own life and the lives of his close friends. No wonder that centuries later Aelred could say, "God is friendship." It is important to realize that this is not a vague statement but carries with it all the concrete ways in which people interdependently share life with each other. To be a friend is to engage in the specifics of relationship: sharing thoughts, feelings, insights, doubts, as well as active care and concern for the well-being of the other. Friendship, then, is not an abstract idea, but the explicit experience of living with and for others, as Jesus said.

This order of friendship is the very core of the marriage relationship. Kenneth Russell, among others, suggests that the demands of marriage (and there are many) are an opportunity to wear away the rough edges of egocentricity and so allow the evolving of true friendship, the friendship Aelred sees as mutual equality and intimacy reaching toward God.

In the Rule of Saint Benedict we find a list of what Benedict calls the tools of good works. They include: to give help in time of trouble; not to give way to anger; not to preserve deceit in one's heart; not to give the kiss of peace insincerely; and to speak with one's mouth the truth that lies in one's heart. The tools also advise one not to be arrogant, not to grumble, not to be a detractor, and to guard one's mouth against evil and vicious speech. One may recognize in this list common-sense guidelines for respectful friendships, and a remarkable applicability to family life.

Friendship between marriage partners, between parents and children (in adult years), and with other family members is a most important part of Christian family life. But for the Christian, the fact of baptism relates one to baptized others at a most profound level, allowing us to reach beyond the natural ties of flesh and blood to those who are different in every way except for their life in Christ. Jesus' teaching about family illustrates this wider experience. Marriage is not an ultimate reality, he says. In heaven there will be no marriage. Some will leave wife and father and home and commitments for the sake of the kingdom, he says. Some things may be more important than family. He identifies those who hear the word of God as his brothers and sisters. His insistence on the penultimate reality of marriage and family has a realistic quality. No other person or persons can fulfill all our needs or claim our total and absolute allegiance. Families that are intent on developing themselves *qua* family face the subtle but grave danger of narcissism on the one hand and idolatry on the other. A good marriage and an ideal family can thus become ends in themselves, fixating people and limiting their capacity to be unself-conscious subjects and agents of genuine evangelization. Friendships with others outside the family have the potential for moving us in wider directions.

The intentional Christian household, mentioned in the introduction, is one way of expanding the intellectual, emotional, and spiritual boundaries of the family. Paula, a young woman I have known for several years, wrote about her growth in such a community. She described it this way:

> I live in an intentional Christian household made up of my husband, Bob, Celia, a young single woman, and myself. We have been together for a little less than six

months now, so it is still new for me. The decision Bob and I made to form a Christian household was motivated by several factors. The principal influence was the fact that we are part of a small prayer group of about twenty-five people, which has one household already, and which views household living as a powerful tool of Christian ministry. The closer the time came to actually do it, the riskier it seemed.

Bob and I had been married only nine months: would our relationship suffer with a third person living with us? Would we have enough privacy? Would I be jealous? Would the three of us get along? I wondered if Celia's standards of cleanliness would mesh with ours, and if she would do her share of the work. I worried about exposing our marriage and our prayer life to someone else's eyes: would we be found lacking?

There is a real fear that we feel when we move out of the nuclear family into something new, and very different. On the most fundamental level, a fear of losing control: of our time, our environment, our relationships. Household living means that we no longer have total control over some of the most basic elements in our lives—what and when we eat, how clean we keep our house, the people that visit us. Someone else's needs and desires in these matters are just as important as our own and must be taken into consideration.

Accepting this was difficult for me. But I am discovering that there is another side to it, one which I feel is very significant. When we lose control or, more to the point, when we learn to give up control—we learn a very important spiritual lesson. We learn to *let go* of many things that we are much better off without, things that constrict us and hinder our growth—and, in the process of letting go, we gain a real freedom.

I am learning to let go of feelings of possessiveness—about my belongings, my time, the house. I am learning that I must let go of the barriers I put up to keep other people at a distance, and allow them to come close, and to know me as I really am, rough edges and all.

I am beginning, too, to glimpse the joy that is also part of living in this kind of family. It is not all struggle. There is the comfort of knowing, experientially, that I am not alone; that my problems and worries are not unique, but shared by others, and thus lessened. There is the strength and creativity that the three of us together can bring to any effort—greater than that any one or two of us could muster. There is the security and confidence of knowing that I am loved and valued, which encourages me to attempt things I would have thought beyond my capabilities before. Most of my fears about household living have been dispelled.

Our household—our family—is a community, where we nurture each other, challenge each other, and help each other to grow. Here we learn about, and teach, the total, accepting love of God, and also the demands that accompany this love. We minister to each other. I sense, too, that it is here that we will be empowered to carry God's love out into the world, to minister to the needs of others. A friend of mine, who also lives in an intentional Christian household, has the theory that the extent to which we share our lives with others is directly proportional to the amount of resources which are then freed up to enable us to minister—resources of time, energy, and money.[13]

Paula and Bob have a baby now. Celia has left. Two unmarried men are living the household experience: sharing household chores, prayer, and various dimensions of social life. To many, these growing households look like new forms of religious community—God's response, perhaps, to the alienation and loneliness of our time.

Another form of friendship with a long and honorable history in the Church is that of spiritual direction. From the beginnings of Christianity this has been recognized as a gift for the welfare of the Church. In this particular focused relationship, a trusted other, one who knows God, waits with a person while God's Spirit rises to new levels of consciousness. During the time of meeting, the director listens and responds in a variety of ways, sensitive to the person and the moment. He or she may offer guidance, encouragement, support, correction, or challenge. As in Aelred's description of friendship, the secrets of the heart are revealed, the quality of life seen, and the stirrings of the Spirit detected and discerned. For married people, a spiritual director for one or both of the partners can help to heighten one's sense of vocation and strengthen one's fidelity to the marital calling.

Tilden Edwards, an Episcopal priest deeply involved in many aspects of spiritual direction, has examined the question of whether wives and husbands can be directors for each other, and has concluded that it is very difficult if not impossible. He writes:

> Though marriage is an important and natural framework for spiritual friendship, there are realistic limitations. Many roles and expectations are involved, and these lurk in the background of more intimate moments. The children are sick, budgets have to be agreed upon, Aunt Jane is coming for a visit. . . . Not only is the marital relationship complicated by such things as those just mentioned, but the partners' spiritual growth often diverges: they move at different paces and in different (though hopefully complementary) directions.[14]

Edwards draws from this the value of a friend or guide or director (the terms may be used interchangeably) outside the marriage, one whose prayerful presence will serve to enrich the marriage and the family. He recognizes that in the Christian tradition, and in other religious traditions as well, celibates often serve as spiritual friends or counselors for married persons. He sees this as complementary:

> Neither marriage nor celibacy is "natural," since both

are vowed states of intentional fidelity that require transmutation of wandering erotic impulses. Both can be training grounds for letting go our slavery to those surprise impulses that can hide, distort and dissipate our responsive awareness to that deeper Ocean of living truth where alone, as Augustine knew, we find our rest.[15]

Contemporary Christian life is marked by a renewal of this ministry. Not only are more members of religious communities serving the larger Christian community as spiritual directors, but lay women and men who are known to be persons of prayer and wisdom are being sought out by others to be spiritual friends. Such intimate friendships offer the opportunity for deep and caring relationships without the expectation of sexual involvement—a rare enough phenomenon in our sexually charged culture. This is not to say that confusion cannot or does not occur. Spiritual awakening and reawakening usually calls forth sexual awakening. We are, after all, sexual beings. An experienced and attuned spiritual director knows this, and knows that for most people integration will follow the awakening. We need only be patient. Like so many aspects of our life in God, waiting is an essential part of this process.

For the better part of seventeen years I have been in spiritual direction. These years have spanned at least two well-documented developmental stages of adult life, that of the young adult who must establish a home and that of the older adult who moves toward expanded commitment to society. Although the shape of my life at these two stages has been different, the content has been basically the same. Over the years there has been the immediate environment of husband, children, parents, friends. There has also been the inner world of thoughts and dreams, images and knowledge. Failure and success—and sin—weave in and out. What I have sought in spiritual direction in all periods of my life has also been basically the same, namely, to realize God in the ongoing events of daily life, to be authentically who I am, to see this *who* as God's creation. I have sought to strike a balance between my dual commitment to domestic life and to professional life.

Throughout the search, a fundamental question persists. It is a question about the meaning of personhood, the meaning of Christian, the force of mission. And always the question contains something about the limits of my generosity and fidelity. Changes in professional and home-life patterns may pose the question in different places and in different ways, but the question is carried with me.

My early experiences in spiritual direction focused mainly on developing spiritual practices, the disciplines necessary for a serious, committed Christian life. The spiritual direction meeting served as a place of accountability as certain disciplines were tried and struggled with, but it was also an uncluttered place to articulate—or to try to articulate—the subtleties of the inner life. In retrospect I can see that this was a vehicle for calling forth hidden parts of my being, illuminating what might be called, in Pauline terms, my gifts, and suggesting the ever-widening prospect of responsibility and choice.

Now, after many years, certain practices (daily intercessory prayer, Scripture, quiet centering, daily Eucharist) are habitual. Less time is given to discussion of the practices as such. Rather, the whole of my life, its breadth and its depth, is the focus. The spiritual direction session remains the uncluttered place where I may see the inner landscape, not only my own but those of the many different people who intersect my life and the corporate life of my family.

Although my spiritual directors have been priests—and though I know the growth that happens in such relationships—I also know that there are limitations to the understanding of one sex for the other. We—men and women—are embodied differently. Our cultural experience is different, even within the Christian subculture. The women's movement has demonstrated the power of women sharing with each other their pain and struggle and hope. Out of this intimate sharing, this trusting of self in the presence of other women, has grown an insistence on equity and justice in society. And the insistence has borne fruit. To be a woman in 1982 is not the same as it was in 1972. Men, too, are beginning to feel their way toward the same liberation that intimate sharing usually enables.

The Cursillo movement, begun under Catholic auspices in Spain in the 1960s and now incorporated into the apostolic life of several Christian denominations, has as part of its structure the regular meeting of friends. The groups, usually four to eight persons, may be all women, all men, or mixed. They usually meet once a week. Each person presents several aspects of his or her current Christian journey: prayer, study, and compassionate Christian action. In an atmosphere of confidential friendship, successes and failures, doubts and faith, may be shared. The friends pray for each other, support and critique each other, and in many ways develop their solidarity with one another. The Cursillo is one way of helping Christian men and women enter into formative, life-giving friendships outside the immediate family grouping. But there are others as well, some of them parish based, some of them spontaneous basic communities.

Final Thoughts

Saint Paul's vision of Christ was the Church, a community of persons with different gifts, living together as intimately connected as the members of the human body. It was this same vision that inspired Benedict to order his households of God, and it is this vision, however indistinct, which draws people to form familial households. We sense the possibility that through the daily living and working together around a common purpose, and through the revelation of self in our closeness to one another, we may discover the pearl of great price within ourselves and within the other.

In her book *Meditations,* Dorothy Day wrote:

True love is delicate and kind, full of gentle perception and understanding, full of beauty and grace, full of joy unutterable. Eye hath not seen nor ear heard, what God hath prepared for those who love Him.

And there should be some flavor of this in all our love for others. We are all one. We are one flesh in the Mystical Body, as man and woman are said to be one flesh in marriage. With such a love one would see all things new; we would begin to see people as they really are, as God sees them.[16]

If the intimacy of family life can cleanse our vision regarding those with whom we share a covenant, might we not hope for the same for all the others who enter our lives? Might we begin to see the stranger as a friend of God?

Chapter 2

EQUALITY

There are no more distinctions between Jew and Gentile, slave and free, male and female, but all of you are one in Christ Jesus.

Galatians 3:28

To the Galatians Saint Paul wrote of the fullness of intimacy, that time when false distinctions of status and worth shall be no more, and all who belong to Christ shall realize their equality as the children of Abraham and heirs of God's promise. Baptism is the great equalizer.

The spiritual life, including as it does increased self-knowledge, interdependent behavior, the acceptance of freedom, and the growing willingness to be gift for others, inevitably leads to an examination of such a fundamental principle as equality. It is not surprising, therefore, that Saint Benedict, early in his Rule, makes quite clear that before God, all are of equal status. David Parry, O.S.B., commenting about this particular section of the Rule of Benedict, writes that the abbot (who has been chosen to head the monastic community) "is to treat all, whether highly born or humbly born, with equal love and care." Abbot Parry goes on to observe that it is one of the great strides forward of our day that social equality has been restored between all members of God's household, meaning, presumably, the monastery. He finally points out—wisely, I think—that law cannot achieve true equality, and it remains a matter of personal application to be borne constantly in mind.[1]

From Galatians to Monte Cassino to the present time has been a long journey, a journey filled with oppression, alienation, and struggle for human dignity and opportunity for all. But the struggle has yielded victories along the way. For example, slavery is now abhorred by all civilized persons and groups, and the rights of men and women are no longer granted according to social class. And there has been growth as well, growth in human and religious consciousness.

In family life both the struggle and the growth have largely centered around the changing roles of women and men, and whether these changes constitute a threat to the welfare of the family. To be mindful of equality is not to seek to break down or diminish all lines of authority in the family. Authority has a crucial role in all group life, as will be discussed in the following chapter. Nor does it mean erasing all differences between men and women. It does mean that within the intimacy of the family, issues of equality between the sexes are being worked through —sometimes with difficulty, often unconsciously, but present nevertheless as part of the dynamics of contemporary family life.

Practical Equality

Much of my own spiritual journey can be told in relation to the fact of the changing roles of men and women and the commitment to equality as a family value. The words I use to identify myself—woman, wife, mother, worker—tell much of the story.

When I met my husband shortly before the opening of Vatican II, the Church was a central reference and rallying point around which we sought to build a common life. There was a lot of ferment and excitement. Change was in the air. At the time of our marriage, my husband was a graduate student, I was a public school teacher, and together we soon became parents: four children in five years.

The first ten years of being wife and mother were, in a way, a time of enclosure. The care of others, the establishment of a home—all the classic developmental tasks of young adulthood —were in the forefront. A serious illness in the early years of marriage became a turning point in *how* I would use this time apart. Because of my illness I could not perform the ordinary activities of homemaking with ease: vacuuming a rug, lifting a baby, preparing a meal all had their price. However, I began to see the situation of that particular period in my life as the gift of limitation and routine. Limited energy meant periods of quiet and opportunities to think, to read, to pray—without feeling guilty for doing nothing.

The illness subsided, but my enclosed routine was continued simply because I wanted it. I had that much power over my life. I was aware that despite four preschool children at home all day, I had much more discretionary use of time than did my husband. I saw that his outside employment allowed me to pursue more directly the education of my soul. Even so, this appreciation of our complementary partnership did not preclude my wanting and needing him to be actively involved in caring for our home and our children. And he wanted to play a central role in parenting during these early years. Time, of course, was a factor for him. Many hours on a demanding job and commuting to and from work left little energy for the nighttime activities of young and enthusiastic children.

Something was askew. Why was the social system so constructed that men had so little time for the journey inward, a journey that for married people includes the building of a home? It seemed to me that, by and large, life demanded much more of married men than simply *being.* The boundaries of their work largely determined their choices.

Social psychologists who have studied the effects of strictly assigned male-female roles conclude that the major tasks of society—government, medicine, education, religion, child rearing—have been without the benefit of full male-female partnership. They particularly note the deprivation of the feminine in the public sectors of society, and the deprivation of the masculine in the home. What has been lost? How can the situation be remedied?

Women: Their Contributions

Dr. Jean Baker Miller[2] believes that women *as a group* have learned a great deal in their enclosed domestic spheres that can be applied to the building of a just and compassionate society. She views women's cooperative, noncompetitive behavior as valuable, but cites as the most important quality—developed through centuries of cultural conditioning—the awareness of feelings of weakness and vulnerability. Although these are feelings common to both men and women, in our society men *as a group* are encouraged to dread, abhor, or deny these feelings, while women are encouraged to cultivate them. All spiritual directors or guides know that such feelings are essential to growth, whether that growth happens through psychotherapy or prayer or both. Dr. Miller writes that the ability to grow psychologically and emotionally requires being in touch with such feelings from time to time. This in-touch-ness is important for life at home and life in business, government, the Church— everywhere. This is very like Saint Benedict's direction about humility (RB 7) which he describes as a descent into the depths of the soul to discover total dependence on God and God's mercy. One might well wonder what would be our fate without these deeply humanizing qualities.

Another quality that has developed among women is creativity, not necessarily in a restricted artistic sense, but in the sense of actively working toward new levels of understanding, which is everyone's life task. For so long now, women with few external outlets for their energy have had to move inward with it, into the realm of soul and spirit. This is why Robert Johnson can say that "women keep a sense of beauty, a sense of connectedness, a sense of at-homeness in the universe that a man doesn't have

. . . a woman discovers what always is."[3] The result has been that women have been engaged in ordinary creativity that enriches daily life, but which we sometimes fail to see because it is always there. They have been arranging homes, cultivating gardens, and nurturing relationships. They have been teaching children and passing on the myths of our civilization. They have been healing the sick with simple, steady physical care. I do not believe that women are now rejecting their own history of creativity as they seek new ways of expression and service. They have known their past offering to be worthwhile, although society as such has rarely given women's creativity external rewards. These rewards have gone elsewhere, to measureable work. This is not so much a question of women having been deprived, as society having been deprived of women's gifts.

Men: New Choices

And what of men? The thrust for equality and balance in the world is not only in terms of women having access to outside work or careers. The impetus for change is also coming from men who notice that something of themselves has been relegated to women, and so lost to them. But now that they've noticed, more and more men acknowledge that they want the nurturing sides of their personalities to emerge. Some are refusing to be merely observers in the central task of life, the rearing of children. Today, men want to be equal participants, not only biologically, but in the continuing act of parenting. The implications of this movement are as revolutionary for the future of the family as Benedict's Rule was for the shaping of Christian monasticism. It is interesting to note that an earlier monastic rule, the Rule of the Master, upon which Benedict built, says that the abbot will show all his disciples and sons the realization of both parents in his own person. He will show his love equally to them as a mother; he shows himself a father to them by uniform tenderness.[4] This reflects the biblical references to God, who is, of course, described as both mother and father.

Dorothy Dinnerstein persuasively argues the importance of the male participation in infant and child care in her book, *The Mermaid and the Minotaur.* She maintains that until and unless fathers are explicitly and concretely engaged in the care of the young, we will not be able to break the strong pull toward sex-determined roles that are largely responsible for inequality in sexual relationships. Without this child-care partnership, she argues, men will continue to believe, however unconsciously or disguisedly, that they are superior; and women, in unconscious, disguised ways, will continue to believe that they are inferior.[5] Children effortlessly learn these attitudes the way they learn language, simply by living with their parents.

Just as women may bring their cultural inheritance and strengths, developed in the privacy of home life, to the public places of work, so men may bring to home and child-care the qualities they have learned and perfected in their work outside the home. Among these I count goal setting and evaluation, thoroughness, analysis, and the concentration and pointedness that allows one to be fully present for a particular task. I do not mean that these qualities are absent in women, but the structure of family life has not yet readily provided an apt environment for them to flourish—just as the world of business and government has not emphasized the value of an aesthetic environment, attention to human relationships, and feelings. The movement toward a more equal and more fully shared life between men and women opens to children the possibility of developing a much broader range of mental, emotional, and social functions that they may later apply to personal and public tasks. This leads me to think about a future where men and women may live at peace with each other, receptive to God's creative power in its many forms and manifestations.

With more and more families achieving equality at home and in the professional and public spheres (through trial and error and often with pain), we are approaching the point of transcending the polarization between feminism and the family, to use Betty Friedan's phrase. How is this happening? I think Carl Jung has helped: more of us are conscious of our inner man or inner woman. For men especially, this seems to be revelatory, as they become less driven and more in touch with emotion, feeling, and mood.[6] Young men grow more reluctant to relegate parts of their personality to women and are more receptive to the variety of contributions that women may make. Young women are refusing to stereotype men and are open about expressing their appreciation of the feminine qualities they perceive in men.

Toward Equality in Work

Work of all kinds has always been essential to the monastic way of life. There is of course the Work of God, the community's prayer of praise, the foundation of all else in the monastic community. But there is also manual labor, performed at regular intervals, just as the Work of God is, and having an importance beyond providing for the community's needs. The work of reading and scholarly study and the work of artisans are also true labor in a monastery. Neither the Rule of Benedict nor the commentaries give any indication that one form of work is more valuable than another, except the Work of God, which all undertake together. This kind of perspective is essential as women and men share their labors within the family, and for the family as they labor in the world. (Freud emphasized that the two most important factors in forming the healthy personality are love and work. Freud's insight is not far from Benedict's Rule, but to my mind, it lacks both the refinements of order and the spirit of egalitarianism.)

For people committed to their families but who also value their work, some significant questions must be addressed. We may agree with the prefatory statement of the Pontifical Council for the Laity that "work must be seen not only as means for persons earning their living, but also as a means for persons to develop their own creative capacities and skills, to take part in the process of building up a more just society as a link whereby people can experience and develop solidarity with others, an opportunity for dialogue, mutual seeking and self-fulfillment— a means of linking the 'social' and the 'private' sides of people's lives."[6] We may also applaud the intervention of the American bishops at the 1980 Synod on the Family, where the bishops noted the fuller sharing of life between men and women. Specifically, they call attention to men and women within the family unit learning to help one another according to their gifts and talents rather than limiting themselves to traditional roles of father and mother. They go on to say that "both are willing to cook, clean, earn money and care for the children. In the broader society also both men and women are developing new skills and confidences in a variety of roles that were once the exclusive domain of one or the other sex. Now both men and women can be doctors and nurses, politicians and scientists, workers and managers."[7] Both these statements are helpful in laying the foundational argument for equality but they overlook the emotional obstacles to be overcome if the full range of equality in work and in life is to be realized.

While our children were small, it never occurred to us to leave their primary care to someone else. I, as the at-home parent, wanted to be involved in their intellectual and spiritual growth. But when they were grown, I felt some new urges within me, a desire to walk some new paths that led away from the home. I had read Simone de Beauvoir in the 1950s (a gift from my husband at our marriage) but I had not yet internalized the issues of women struggling for equality and autonomy that de Beauvoir so superbly described.

My new restlessness was channeled into graduate school. This experience, undertaken some fifteen years ago, parallels the stories of many women whose personal movement preceded the organized women's movement. This new undertaking, while exhilarating and clearly satisfying my need for work other than housework, also released the cultural accumulation of generations of assigned sexual roles: no amount of de Beauvoir could dissuade me from trying to be superwoman, nor could it enable a supportive husband, intellectually in agreement with all the aspects of equality, to start thinking like a housewife. He would —and did—help as long as I thought of what needed to be done. Later, a part-time job with career commitments didn't alleviate the situation very much. For a long time, only I knew whether there was enough milk for dinner. Other areas of life we worked out with relative ease: we agreed on who would attend school conferences and who would bring the oranges to the soccer games. It wasn't until I moved into full-time employment, which we both somehow perceived as "equal work," that we could see clearly how unequal our sharing of home responsibilities had been. The real problem was that I *felt* responsible for all the details of domestic life, a pattern that lingered from the time when our labors were more definitely separate.

As we talked about equitable sharing of homemaking duties, we realized that we needed to learn how to share the executive functions of running a household. We had to unlearn and relearn. I had to wait—and not continually step in and fix things up. My husband said frankly that if I always attended to the daily needs of family living, he would never learn to see and sense what was needed. So some evenings there was no milk, but the family began to shape a new way of being community, a way suited to shifting responsibilities.

To reach this point of seriously working on sharing life at home and labor outside the home we have had to be honest with each other. We have had to assess how much we value each other's outside work, not only in monetary terms, but in other terms as well. This has meant examining our consciences, in a way, to see what we really think and feel about each other's contribution to the world. We have had to discuss freely how we regard household tasks, how much we respect our work at home, what we think we're best suited for, what we're willing to learn. Obviously our now young-adult children have had to be involved in these conversations because they, too, share in much of the adult decision making. They see that we are all balancing many responsibilities.

Our prayer these days frequently includes gratitude for God's confidence in us as stewards of many treasures. We also pray for the grace to speak to each other in a true spirit of fraternal correction whenever the demons of dominance-subservience intrude and equality becomes distorted. Attention to equality is not, however, disregard of service. Service is at the center of Christian life, but so is freedom to choose.

In an earlier age, monasticism offered to men and women an alternative to life in a world that was marked by inequality of birth and station and money. The monastery, with a life-style fashioned on order and equality, rendered a new kind of freedom for persons. This did not go unnoticed by the world.

In our time, the family embodies an alternative model for transcending the polarities which Saint Paul enumerates in the letter to the Galatians. The Christian family carries within it the biblical strain that affirms that in Christ there is neither slave nor free, male nor female, but a profound unity. The challenge to the Christian family is the same as the challenge to the Church: to be faithful to Jesus' instruction that we are to be in the world but not of it (John 17).

It would be helpful to families, however, if the Church would speak out on their behalf with regard to the social changes that will be necessary if there is to be genuine equality in the home and in the workplace. The Church might speak unambiguously about: the value of both parents sharing in infant and child care; the importance of meaningful work for a developed Christian life; the need to shape new patterns of work and family life, so that both the family and society can benefit from the partnership of men and women. Furthermore, the Church might suggest practical steps for companies to take: parental leave (so that both parents may be with their infants), part-time jobs with benefits, job sharing, and so on.

As men and women move toward fully shared parenting and participation in the world of work, some important life-style changes in families are likely to occur. A simpler way of living must be expected. Adjusted economic standards will be necessary. Benedict's Rule, which favors consuming only that which is needed (as opposed to unlimited consumption of the world's resources) is once again relevant. Already there are families that have made decisions along these lines.

Isabella and Steve are both professional musicians. They are also conscientious parents of two children. From the beginning of their marriage and parenthood they knew that if they were to honor the gift of their musical talent, as well as honor their vocation as parents, they would have to make some far-reaching decisions about shared responsibility.

Isabella is a pianist and singer; Steve is a clarinetist. He performs and she teaches—this was their first decision. They say they both could not be full-time performers and still be faithful to their children. Isabella's musical interests lie in how sound and music affect and form people. She doesn't want to sing to applause so much as to carry on a musical conversation. She's also concerned about the demands of the ego that are inevitable in a successful performer. Steve loves to play music—it is that simple. Their decision as to who would concentrate on performing seemed to flow from who they are as persons.

Other decisions were not so naturally arrived at. Economics, for example. Isabella and Steve live on *one* full income, derived from their part-time work, in a city and neighborhood where the middle class standards usually require two full incomes. They were helped in working through the rightness and the logistics of this decision through the support of their small but energetic and risk-taking Episcopal congregation. Fellow parishoners cared enough about Steve and Isabella's Christian call to music and to family to take time to pray with them and talk with them so that they could sort through all the ramifications of their life-style.

While the children were preschoolers, Isabella did not see her private pupils at home. She and Steve felt the children had some rights in their home. They needed to be able to come and go in some normal fashion. Steve's presence at home during the day, and the openness of a nearby church that lent her a room and a piano, made it possible for Isabella to develop her teaching career. She still performs, but not for critics. She leaves that to Steve. Her performances are in old persons' homes where she has participatory concerts, and in colleges, where young women want to discuss the ways and means of parenthood and career.

Steve and Isabella say that sharing of household and child care has taught them a valuable spiritual lesson: that of letting go. Each has had to let go of insisting on her or his way of shopping, preparing food, house management, child management; they have learned to trust each other's differences and respect each other's sincerity. They are helped in this by their love of music, their belief that "the life of sound has no limits, no boundaries. The life of sound is not limited to the mind." Through their work they are moving deeper and deeper into the spaciousness of God. Equality and shared responsibility are their vehicles.

Some years ago I stood in the Sistine Chapel for the first time, overwhelmed by the sweep of Michelangelo's all-encompassing mural. I stared at the garden: the snake, symbolic of sin and rupture, is entwined around the tree of knowledge of good and evil. On one side is Adam; on the other is Eve. Adam is looking backward across the tree to Eve, and reaching out to her as if to bridge, somehow, the gulf between them. But it is too great a distance, or so it seems. He cannot reach her. As I stood before the scene I thought, "Genesis is unfinished." I thought about the beginnings of the human story, the Creation accounts that speak of man and woman as together created in the image of God. (Gen. 1:27). I thought about the fact that Jesus called both women and men to be his friends and followers. Catholic social teaching also came to mind, especially the documents of Vatican II that speak unequivocally for equality between men and women. And yet if there is agreement that man and woman do enjoy an intrinsic equality and interdependent partnership, then why, I wondered, has there been such a severe separation between them? Why has there been such widespread cultural approval across time and space of those high walls that have prevented the full cooperation and participation of women and men in all phases of their mutual concerns and common life?[8]

I continue to wonder if the adherence across time and cultures to rigid sex-role assignments, which have usually placed women in enforced subservience and men in equally enforced dominant and competitive roles, is not the result of this original brokenness. Is our participation in redemption to be the finishing of Genesis?

Theological reflection, sociological and psychological insights, the Christian spiritual heritage, are all conveyers of the rightness of equality between men and women. The Christian family, grounded as it is in self-giving love, is likely to be a trustworthy place to work at the arduous task of authentic equality, not only for the benefit of the family, but for the world. The family is a privileged arena where true equality in the context of responsibility can be practiced for the benefit of the larger community.

As this work goes forward, we might keep in mind the words of the American bishops at the 1980 synod. They courageously proclaimed that "co-equality, interdependence and complementarity of men and women in marriage and in the institutions of society is the will of God."[9] This has to be, then, a serious matter for our individual and collective examination of conscience.

Chapter 3

AUTHORITY

His teaching made a deep impression on them because he spoke with authority.

Luke 4:32

We hear a great deal today about the breakdown in familial authority, or more precisely parental authority. Parents seem to have lost control over their children and are able to say little about how they should dress or behave or who their friends will be or who they will marry. Are we facing a crisis of authority?

There was a time when family expectations carried a great deal of weight. Not only did small children dress and speak and keep silent according to parental directions, but young men and women often moved along parentally approved vocational paths. Young men followed the family business or embarked on appropriate careers. In Irish families it was not uncommon to "give" one son to the Church as a priest and to keep one daughter at home to care for elderly parents. Marriage usually required family consent, for marriage was of too great consequence to be left to the young.

Interfaith marriages, which were often interethnic as well, were discouraged, if not outrightly forbidden. Who can forget the sorrowful comment of Tevya, the Jewish father in *Fiddler on the Roof,* when his daughter leaves home to marry a Gentile. With all the piercing reality of genuine grief he flatly states, "She is dead to us." And so it was.

48

When I was growing up interfaith marriages carried for Catholics and Protestants and Jews the risk of parental and family disapproval and even exclusion. These attitudes preserved the continuity of particular religious and cultural heritages. Tevya was right: the life of the family in that period depended on tradition. And something has been lost with the passing of this kind of dependability. On the other hand, there is a sense of relief that the Victorian patriarch has all but disappeared. Authoritarianism no longer holds absolute rule over the lives of women and children. Members of families enjoy the freedom to exercise a wide range of choice: whether to marry, and if so, whom; which career to follow. What, then, constitutes the crisis?

To me, the crisis grows out of this period of social change, a period in which authority is being redefined and experienced in new ways under the principles of equality. Christian families of all kinds, the traditional family, the one-parent family, the intentional household family, are all affected by society's efforts to come to some agreement about the nature of authority and its proper function in the lives of men, women, and children.

In all spheres of group life today, in government, business organizations, and even the Church, there is a growing awareness that the common life of the group is best conducted not in an autocratic way, but by some form of shared responsibility. This sounds simpler than perhaps it really is. But to Americans, whose civil life is grounded in democratic procedures, there is a rightness to it. And for Catholics, shared responsibility is the outstanding issue with respect to how the Church will be governed in the spirit of Vatican II. So, too, for families in our time. It is particularly relevant for parents who want to teach their children the ways of responsible citizenship in both society and Church, but who want to do so with respect for the genuine values found in cultural pluralism, as well as for the values found in their religious traditions. And they want to do this with respect for individual autonomy. What, then, are reasonable patterns for Christian parental authority and shared responsibility?

Authority and Shared Responsibility: The Monastery and the Home

In Benedict's Rule the place of the abbot is pivotal since he is believed to be chosen by the monastic community to serve in Christ's stead. The qualities for such a person are discussed early in the Rule. Obviously, the right order and harmonious functioning of the household depend largely on how the abbot carries out his duties.

The Rule's suggestions as to how authority should be exercised and the enumeration of the qualities desirable in the abbot are rich in possibilities for parental meditation. The monastic households mirror a number of insights concerning the exercise of authority in families. The depth of human understanding found in the Rule is attested by the fact that it still bears a common-sense relevance for Christian families today.

First of all, the Rule states that the abbot should be well instructed in the ways of the Gospel and the knowledge and love of Christ, and he should also be mindful of the responsibility he has *willingly* undertaken. The decision for parenthood requires as much serious reflection as does the acceptance of the call to be an abbot. Responsible parenthood, at the very least, requires a clear understanding that the biological role is only one part of the total parental enterprise. With the birth of the first child, a married couple undergoes a transition from being simply a married couple to being new parents. For many people parenthood is existentially the irrevocable sign of permanent commitment.[1] Like the abbot, a parent knows that he or she now bears a burden that requires wisdom, compassion, and learning.

Christian parents are charged with imparting a world view to their children; as lay people in the Church, they are a crossroad for their children between culture and Gospel.

From infancy on, parents create for a child an environment

that flows from the totality of their being. Their spiritual and secular values are simply there, in the family, and they are to a large degree absorbed by the children. This is especially true of Gospel values, which, to the degree that they are active, form the core of spiritual awareness and ethical behavior. Other life values, like art and music, science, love of nature, political concern, and so forth, are also passed on largely to the extent that they are embodied in the home environment. There are, however, other vehicles for socialization in secular values. But it is the family as domestic church, even more than the parish, that can and does impart the Gospel during the earliest period of a person's life.

Saint Benedict indicates that the abbot is to point out to those in his charge all that is good and holy *more by example than by words,* demonstrating God's instructions by a *living example.* As in the monastery, our children clearly know what we value by what we do and how we do it. If the Eucharist is the central nourishment in our lives, they know. If Sunday Mass is a heavy burden for us, they know. If the Scriptures are life-giving words to us, they know. They see us, as husband and wife, comfort each other in our low moments. They see us unable or unwilling to enter each other's place of sorrow. They see us forgive each other our sins, and watch us bridging estrangements and coming home to each other. They know whether we respect each other's solitude and privacy or whether we are threatened by that. They are with us when we welcome the stranger, and when we do not. By living with us they know how and to what degree we share our abundance and our need with others. I believe that what we most want to hand on to our children in best done by working on that within ourselves.

Children of divorced parents can see that they, the children, are persons of incalculable worth if they see their separated parents continue to find ways to be responsible to those to whom they have given life. They will know how difficult this continuing care can be when the natural support of marital intimacy is not there to help in the role of parenting. A child who lives with a single parent can come to know that the parent lives sustained by faith and hope, and by a love that is capable of transcending personal loneliness.

No spoken words can convey one's truth, one's belief system, one's world view so much as these life-words lived out day by day in ordinary families.

This is not to dismiss what we commonly think of as teaching or correction within the family. Growing children need boundaries and instruction. This offers opportunities for genuine parental creativity and personal growth. Benedict wisely wrote that the abbot must understand the difficulty of a variety of temperaments and accommodate and adapt himself to each one's character and intelligence (RB 2:32); he should employ a variety of suitable methods for teaching those entrusted to his care. Against this background parental authority can be understood as active care and love.

In order to appreciate the variety of temperaments in our families, and to search carefully for the right way to communicate with different members, parents need to concentrate on and study the different personalities. This concentration becomes part of the instructive and corrective process. We ponder our child. We try to see beyond appearances (listlessness, defiance, bravado) to the heart of the person, to the center of human need and desire expressed in that child or young person. We concentrate to see how best to communicate the truth we know and the love we bear. This is, in fact, a form of contemplation, a nonanalytic approach to parental authority. The contemplation begins in the free will of the parent, in the desire to turn toward the child and the willingness to be present to those whose life has come from us, or to those whom we've chosen by adoption. We learn from this contemplative presence. We learn about the uniqueness of the child, about our own unresolved, often hidden conflicts, and about the ever-present mysterious action of grace.

The practice of authority that flows from recognition of others' needs requires time: time to study and pray for the family members, time for self-study, and time for family interaction and communication.

Shared Responsibility

One of the distinguishing marks of the abbot's authority is his seeking the counsel of others. "As often as anything important is to be done in the monastery, the abbot shall call the whole community together and explain what the business is, and after hearing the advice of the brothers, let him ponder it and follow what he judges the wiser course" (RB 3:17). The commentary on the Rule explains that this is not really an exercise in parliamentary democracy, but rather a community consultation, a gathering to try to discern the will of God. This is, of course, the way of the New Testament Church, where the Spirit is given to the community. In Benedictine life, where even the youngest member is respected as one called by God to live in this particular community, a model for family consultation is found.

One form of family consultation is found in the work of Rudolph Dreikers, who developed the idea of family council. This is a gathering of all members of the family in a structured way to communicate concerns, hopes, plans, and problems. It is a way of giving all, even the youngest, a voice. It provides a forum for decisions. Christian family councils that incorporate prayer into their gathering can and do become ways of discerning God's will for the family.

Two stories of Christian family consultation come to mind. One is a story of my own household and the other is a story of a family I know well.

Some years ago when I was in graduate school preparing for comprehensive examinations, I began to feel as if I were drowning in multiple and diverse duties. At the time I was meeting weekly with two other women for Scripture, life-sharing, and prayer. In the middle of one of our meetings, a torrent of incoherent anxiety and resentment mixed with tears rushed out of me. I was so close to my own crisis I couldn't see that I was at the edge of exhaustion trying to prepare for exams and trying to maintain a household that went on "as usual." One of my friends, a political activist, grabbed a campaign poster from her current stack, turned it over and wrote on the back in large red letters, "Please Help." Quietly and firmly she told me to hang this signal on my refrigerator door. I did. That night at dinner my husband suggested that in an hour or so we all sit down again (our children were then eight, ten, eleven, and twelve years old) and discuss mother's problem. The basic message had already been given, and received. I needed help. How the family would share that burden was the subject for discussion. Just knowing that my family now knew how I felt was a partial solution. The discernment led the children to see they were needed in new ways at this time in our family life, and that there were extra practical chores that they could do. Their father led the way in picking up household responsibilities. I felt the freedom to let go of certain standards of housekeeping that simply had to be set aside, and haven't been missed by the family.

This experience of consultation and consequent shared responsibility for the home conveyed to our children, I think, that their contributions were genuinely needed by the family. This was the first time, although not the last, that their responsible participation in the life of our family has been a form of ministry. They have been called upon from time to time, especially when their father has been seriously ill, to assume authority in certain spheres. And they have been reliable and strong tenders of family and home when that's been needed. This has been an echo to me of Benedict's observation that the Lord often reveals what is better to the younger.

A friend of mine—I will call her Elinor—is divorced and the mother of two teenage children. For a long time she has held a deep and personal belief in her vocation to a simple life-style, living in the center of the city and working side by side with the ethnic groups that cities attract. The family has lived in the inner city for six years. The children share their mother's active concern for social justice and have valued the experience of explicit Christian life that this has meant. The older child is away at college now. For some time, Elinor has had the growing feeling that she should move out of the inner city to a newer apartment. Being a woman of prayer, she has wrestled with her reasons. The city apartment is untolerably hot in the summer, but she manages with the help of fans. Her street is noisy and it is difficult for her to sleep, but that's only a problem in the summer when the windows are open. She has to search for a parking place on the street for her car, but she usually finds one. One day she said to me, "I want to open my door and see something beautiful. And I want a kitchen counter. It doesn't make sense." But as she consulted with her community—her friends, her confessor, her children—it began to make sense.

Her life is now developing along a path different from when she made her move to the city. She is a professional in the Church, and the demands on her time and energy are considerable. She is facing one of the questions of middle age: does she have sufficient personal resources to meet the demands of complex and trying urban life and the demands of her professional full-time ministry? Is God calling her to a new place? Conversations with her adult communities refined her questions. Her consultation with her children resulted in two different opinions. Her college-age child favors the move; her younger child prefers to stay in the city, even though this move will not mean a change of school. Like the abbot, however, the decision finally rested with Elinor. The family will move and Elinor's daughter is adjusting to the idea. All who know Elinor, including her children, know that she lives under a higher authority. This evokes respect for her decisions, if not easy agreement.

Authority, Responsibility, and Gifts

Saint Paul's vision of the Church grew around a theology of gifts. He saw the Church as a body, an organism whose members have been given different gifts for the good of all. Some recent theological development of the notion of gifts, service, and ministries takes note of the unique form a gift may take in a person or in a community.[2] The family, as a domestic church, participates in this vision and reality of giftedness. Furthermore, there is a correlation between authority in the family and the gifts that reside in a particular family. When children are young, parents committed to the principles of equality as described in chapter 2, and to the theology of giftedness, will try to work out their parental responsibilities in ways that benefit both the children and themselves. Gifts that are exercised grow. Parents who are in touch with their own giftedness are likely to be disposed toward evoking and affirming the gifts they see in their children, even if the gifts are hidden like seeds in the ground, or if they seem to be strange and unconnected gifts.

When I was a young wife and mother I met a family consisting of wife, husband, and ten children. Theirs was a household where everyday creativity was encouraged. I don't mean creativity in the strict sense of sculpting or painting. That was there, and rope sculpture did indeed hang from the chandelier because one son was (and is today) an artist. But I mean this more in terms of the value that was placed on the life-work unfolding in each one, including the parents. I remember the parents rejoicing over one boy's carpentry skills (he's now a furniture maker), one girl's struggle to be a lawyer (and now she is), another boy's itinerant adventures as an apple picker, where he learned all about apples and more about life on the road. These parents were obviously as proud of their plumber son as of their literary daughter. A rich variety of gifts and of life-work was able to develop in this family environment because the family community affirmed the gifts as equal in value for the sake of the world. This, too, reflects the monastic attitude. The prologue to Benedict's Rule acknowledges that God's good gifts are present in the community, and later in the *Rule,* the abbot is cautioned against favoritism. As the organizational plan of the monastic life unfolds, one sees how the various roles are regarded. Abbot Parry, commenting on the Rule,[3] reminds us that all human situations, actions, and undertakings may be directed toward the glory of God. This avoids the dualism of dividing life simply into the sacred and the profane. Parry recalls that in the Old Testament the skill and perception and knowledge of every kind of craft was seen as a divine gift (Exod. 31:24).

This reverence for each one's giftedness reflects a particular kind of authority, that of competency. But competency bears watching. Not only do particular competencies develop in some family members, in others they decline. This is especially evident as parents grow older, and roles may be reversed. Children, when they reach mid-life, may find themselves caring for their parents and exercising the kind of authority that they experienced as children.

There are two sayings from the religious traditions of the East that summarize the attitudes of parents and children. They are particularly applicable as authority shifts in the household. One is an ancient Chinese saying and refers to duties toward children and posterity: "Great reverence is owed to a child." The other is from Hindu wisdom and refers to duties toward parents and elders: "Your father is an image of the Lord of Creation, your mother is an image of the Earth. For him who fails to honor them, every work of piety is in vain. This is the first duty."[4]

A Checklist for Household Authority

Saint Benedict's ideas concerning the abbot's role in the community are rich in wisdom for the conduct of authority in family households. Always the emphasis is on the authentic example of the abbot:

He must be chaste, temperate and merciful.
He should always let mercy triumph over judgment.
When he must punish, he should use prudence and
avoid extremes; otherwise by rubbing too hard to
remove the rust, he may break the vessel.
He is to distrust his own fraility, and remember
not to crush the bruised reed.

However, he should not allow faults to flourish, but rather:

He should prune them away with prudence and love
as he sees best for each individual.
Let him strive to be loved, rather than feared.
Excitable, anxious, extreme, obstinate, jealous
or oversuspicious he must not be. Instead, he
must show forethought and consideration. Whether the
task he assigns concerns God or the world,
he should be discerning and moderate.
Finally, he must so arrange everything that the
strong have something to yearn for and the weak
nothing to run from. [RB 64]

Parents, and all of us who are responsible in any way for the well-being of others, could make use of this list as a stimulus, a beginning, to reflect on how we are in fact transmitting life and educating those committed to our care.

Nevertheless, despite discerning, generous, and judicious parental authority, despite a commitment to shared responsibility within the household, despite the steady and fair expression of love within the home, some children, especially in the tumultuous adolescent years, reject all bonds of family love and law. Christian parents can feel enormous guilt when all their efforts at helping their son or daughter and all the disciplinary measures seem to fail. Normal parental reaction is, "How have we failed?" This sense of guilt is understandable but not appropriate for Christians who realize that the ongoing redemptive adventure includes free will, in our children as well as in ourselves. It includes sin and failure, repentance and reconciliation. We all tend to measure life in our restrictive category of time, and consequently forget that how and when our lost children will be found and received by Christ is known only to him. In the meantime, wise, prudent, and merciful parental responsibility sometimes includes apparently harsh actions. One family I know had to declare a delinquent son beyond their control. They came to this decision after many serious attempts to help him limit his behavior were ineffective. This, too, was foreseen in Benedict's Rule. He recognized that some monks would have to be excommunicated after all attempts at reform were unsuccessful. These monks had to be separated from the common life of the monastery for the good of all. The monastery though was not judged a failure because of the wayward brother, nor was the brother totally rejected. Rather, love for him was reaffirmed (2 Cor. 2:8), and all continued to pray for him. As for the abbot, he was to imitate the loving example of the Good Shepherd, who left the ninety-nine sheep in the mountains and went in search of the one sheep that had strayed. So great was his compassion for its weakness that he mercifully carried it on his sacred shoulders back to the flock (Luke 15:5, in RB 27:8–9).

Families and Gospel Authority

Jesus spoke with authority and the people were impressed. This is how Jesus is remembered in Luke's Gospel. What did the people perceive in Jesus when they insisted, "This man has authority"?

Have you ever heard a person speak about a topic and known without a doubt that the truth was spoken? Or have you been in the presence of one who had probed the depths of his or her own experience, and known that this person was in touch with the wellsprings of life? When such a person speaks to you, a certain pure power is conveyed. Integrity and authenticity are present. Such a person reads the human heart, as Jesus did. "There was no need for anyone to tell him about men because he knew what was in their hearts" (John 2:25). This kind of authenticity and authority penetrates our human defenses and reaches into the center of our souls, urging us to shed all the veils that shield us from God's love, and from freedom.

It is interesting to me that Jesus' authoritative way is mentioned shortly after his first public appearance in Nazareth, his home. It happens early in his ministry. He goes to the synagogue on the Sabbath, takes the scroll, and chooses to read the following words of Isaiah:

> The Spirit of the Lord has been given to me
> for he has annointed me
> He has sent me to bring the good news to the poor
> to proclaim liberty to captives
> and to the blind new sight
> to set the downtrodden free,
> to proclaim the Lord's year of favor.
>
> Luke 4:18–19

This is a freedom passage. Here, in the fourth chapter of Luke, freedom and authority are linked. Jesus' authority is associated with integrity, authenticity, and liberation. It is also associated with the service of others.

Jesus himself directly spoke about the use of authority. He did so at the end of his earthly life, on the night before he died. Words spoken at such moments have, I think, singular importance in the mind of the speaker. Time is running out. Nonessentials are sifted out. To his close friends, and to his Church, Jesus said:

> Among pagans it is the kings who lord it over them, and those who have authority over them are given the title Benefactor. This must not happen with you. No. The greatest among you must behave as if he were the youngest, the leader as if he were the one who serves. For who is greater: the one at table or the one who serves?

The one at table surely. Yet here am I among you as one who serves.

Luke 22:25–27

The final teaching of Jesus on the use of authority places it definitively in the realm of service and humility.

Authority, in Gospel terms, is not the capricious use of power or the desire to control others for the sake of control. Instead, it is love in action, teaching a way of life; it is intended to guide the young toward mature liberty. For parents, for all who guide the young, and for those who bear a responsibility for others, our own continuing adult formation is the greatest guarantor of true authority. A central pathway for this formation is the path of prayer.

Chapter 4

PRAYER

I fall on my knees before the Father, from whom every family in heaven and on earth receives its true name. I ask God, from the wealth of his glory, to give you power through his Spirit to be strong in your inner selves.

Ephesians 3:14–16

My husband and I brought our firstborn home, alone. No grandparents or relatives or friends were standing by to tell us if she was breathing normally, or if she would live through the night. We set the alarm for 2 A.M. in order to feed her on time, afraid she would grow weak without regular nourishment. We worked very hard—both of us—at caring for this new life. I, particularly, was mortally afraid for her physical well-being. I wanted to shield her from germs and from anything that might harm her. I prayed that she would get a little bigger and a little stronger and a little older—fast—so I could relax.

Years and children later, my focus has shifted. I still want to shield my own from all harm, and now I know more about the variety of harm that is possible. Antibiotics can conquer germs, but what of the principalities and powers that wait ready to contend with every man and woman? What protection can I offer my children against such danger? Only that which fortifies me in my own daily combat with darkness and distortion, that is, the mercy of God, mercy abundantly given for the asking. That is why the prayer of Ephesians has been my prayer for the family given to me. Daily I ask God from the wealth of his glory to give them power through his Spirit that they may be strong in their inner selves. I include in this prayer all who might be called family: those who abide in our household, those who live at a distance, and those who come to be with us for only a little while and who strengthen our inner selves. For how else can we dare to live truthful and generous lives in the face of all the imponderables and ambiguities, in the midst of all the suffering and absurdity? How else except that our inner persons grow strong, becoming like Christ?

Prayer: Christian Foundation

Prayer permeates our scriptural and historical heritage. The Gospel portrays Jesus as a man of prayer, privately and publicly. He went to lonely places to be with God. He joined the congregations in common prayer. He taught others how to pray, for that is what his followers asked of him. Teach us how to pray they asked, not what to pray. The Lord's Prayer, then, is not so much a prayer as a set of attitudes for prayer and for life.

The primitive Christian Church followed Jesus' example and fostered both private and communal prayer. One source indicates that Christians were to pray the Lord's Prayer three times a day.[1] Later the custom of praying at particular times—at the third, sixth, and ninth hours of the day, as well as at morning, evening, and night—became rather firmly established. These set times had associative links with Christ's passion and death, and they carried over into the desert monasteries and finally into the patterns of psalms, prayers, readings, and hymns so central to Benedictine households.

The Office, or the Work of God, was intended primarily as the praise of the Creator, and this remains its essential characteristic. While the gatherings of the monks to sing God's praises is the Work of God, and this common prayer shapes the consciousness of the monastic family, the prayer is intended to be continued privately in interior prayer as the communion of the soul with God. The community's praise is to go on in the silence of each person's solitary prayer.[2]

Daily Anchors

People often speak of feeling themselves torn to bits and pieces. Families carried along on a tide of activity and involvement can and do feel fractured, uncentered, and plain worn out. Adult members go to jobs or to school (sometimes both), manage a home, tend children and gardens, chauffer youngsters to their many activities, try to be responsible citizens of the political community, the school community, the church community. Children, too, feel pressure at an early age, the pressure to participate. Group life is considered more important than solitary activity. Yet most families do have some structure, which allows them to manage with some sense of order and security. There are evening meals, which for most families constitute a family gathering. Expectations also serve as structures: perhaps everyone knows that lunches are to be taken to school or work. Music lessons once a week, grocery shopping on Saturday, Church on Sunday. The natural structures of family life provide for moments of community, for the being together that is vital to a family's health and well-being. These times of recognizing family identity can be moments of family worship. The sacramental life of the members affects this: their baptism and confirmation, their participation in the eucharistic community, the parents' sacrament of marriage—all mark these ordinary communal events as moments in God.

Enumerated in the Rule are many details for ordered living, for example, what and when to eat and drink, what to wear, how to sleep, and, of course, when and how to pray. Many of these concrete directives are no longer applicable to contemporary monastic life, and they have even less relationship to contemporary family life. Some similar order, some kind of reliable daily ritual is necessary, however, if we are to grow in prayer and live in peace. Imagine what contemporary home life would be like without the minimal structures and anchors that have been mentioned. Structure and spontaneity—both are important to a fully developed life. Artists know that routine means freedom to create, but they also know the joy of unplanned expression. Parents know that discipline and routine help family security, but they also know exceptions allow for growth. Prayer, too, benefits from both structure and spontaneity.

Common Prayer

The family as a worshipping community has tended to be lost in ordinary Christian life, at least in ordinary Catholic Christian life. The parish is what we think of when we use the term worship. Yet the Judaic strains in our tradition emphasize the home and the family as the center of prayer. "Not only prayer but liturgy proper is, in Judaism, validly undertaken in the home setting. Every week, when the mother lights the Sabbath candles, when the blessings are uttered and the songs are sung to welcome the Sabbath bride, the Jewish home is consecrated anew as a sacred place. In our Christian terminology, the home becomes for the Sabbath and the feasts celebrated there, a Church, the point of contact between the whole people and God."[3] However, without the custom of family prayer and liturgy as it exists in the Jewish home, Christian families may often wonder how to start.

The practice of family prayer best begins, I believe, when children are infants. Just as babies know they can rely on their parents for food and affection, they can come to expect that praise, thanksgiving, petition—that explicit recognition of the Holy One—will be in their family. The very first step of common prayer in the life of a young family is for the wife and husband to be together, at some time in the day, in some kind of prayer. It may be the Lord's Prayer prayed aloud. It may be a short period of silent prayer. Whatever it is, infants are aware of it because prayer itself is a presence.

Children begin to know us as soon as they enter our world.

It is a natural next step to incorporate young children into the prayer moments. It seems to me that there is something instinctively right about the basic monastic prayer rhythms of morning, evening, and night. Every religious tradition takes notice of these natural daily rhythms to remember the One who created us and breathes life into us for yet another day. So for a family, morning prayer, however brief and unadorned, does create awareness about who we are and where our trust ultimately lies. It leads us into the day with a little more genuine humanity than if we begin with only the morning papers.

Mornings in most families are frantic. However, a few minutes at breakfast in silent prayer can break the chain of frenzy. Touching each other in a spirit of prayer can be a short but important moment of affirmation at the beginning of a day that promises its full share of stress at the office, at school, in household management. During one difficult period in my life when I was feeling much inner turmoil, my husband would hold me close and simply ask God to be with me that day. That brief ordinary ministry was like an anointing to me. From time to time we share a similar kind of morning prayer, physically, with each other. Now it includes thanksgiving. We've been saved so often.

Another form of regular morning prayer long favored in our family was that of blessing our children as they left for school. My husband and I each had our own style. I would mark the cross on the forehead of each child with some brief prayer as each went out the door. Their father usually placed his hands on the children's heads, stilling them for a minute and praying silently for their welfare.

I have heard of other families where everyone rises early for Scripture and meditation, but they must be families with disciplined parents and willing and compliant children.

The evening meal is a natural occasion for family prayer and a natural point in the day to once again acknowledge the Christ in whom we live and move and have our being (Acts 17). With small children evening prayer will need to be brief, perhaps a simple grace or a parent-led blessing. As children grow older, particularly in preadolescence, spontaneous prayer at meals happens naturally and often provides a vehicle for releasing all kinds of feelings. I have noticed in my own family an interesting shift in this regard. As the children moved into adolescence there was little, if any, spontaneous prayer. I associated this new reticence with the maelstrom within them as they moved unevenly toward emotional maturity.

From their earliest childhood days, it had been our custom to use the prayer of the Church at mealtimes on the great feasts: morning prayer at Easter and Christmas breakfast; vespers at Christmas dinner, family birthdays, and baptismal anniversaries, which we always celebrated. I remembered the calming effect of this ritual prayer on such occasions. It seemed to me that some formality was needed in our prayer, something steady and reliable. So during the children's adolescence we relied on the Psalms for our evening prayer: one Psalm and a ritual grace. I think the young men and women around our dinner table appreciated being carried along by something older, wiser, and stronger than themselves, by prayer that had been used by others who had gone before them and had survived.

The liturgical seasons are special gifts to families who want to develop a life of common prayer. Young children particularly respond to the anticipatory rituals of Advent, the celebrations of Christmas, the sparseness of Lent, and the fruitfulness of Easter, and the community spirit of Pentecost. The parish, or the basic Christian community, is a valuable resource for supporting the family in its attempts to pray at these occasions together.[4] Parents can learn a great deal from preparing these celebrations with and for their children.

Nontraditional families, say, a single parent with children or a community of young people, are perhaps more challenged to create their own rituals than the more traditional kinds of families who are carried along by the cultural currents. One single parent I know each year faces a number of options for celebrating Christmas. This parent, especially sensitive to the subtleties of the Lord's leadings in his family's life, consults with the children (now adolescents) about how best to celebrate Christ's birth *this* year. Should we accept an invitation to be with friends on Christmas Day? Should we invite some single people to our home? Should we join with other Christian activists in a day of service to the poor? All kinds of options and celebrations have been part of this family's common prayer life. Their nontraditional situation has been an opportunity rather than a liability. Each Christmas and Easter requires thought, prayer, preparation, choice.

The common events of every family's life—the ordinary time —offer possibilities for prayer. The preparation of food is one example. Some parents pray aloud for peace as they prepare meals. One father I know reminds his children that, in a way, everything that nourishes them has died for them, so that they might be fed and live. His children seem to have a sense of gratitude about it all. Dinner parties in our home are a joint enterprise. As my husband and I prepare the food for our guests we often pray for them as well, nothing elaborate or sustained, simply a blessing on those who will join us in the meal.

Waiting is another part of ordinary time. We are always waiting. We wait for people, we wait for news, we wait for the phone to ring, we wait on lines. Two or three people waiting together in peaceful quiet awareness change the quality of the waiting. We can then wait with openness, with less grasping, more in touch with the present moment.

Illness, to some degree, is part of every family. Most of us are not heroic enough to really welcome illness as participation in Christ's suffering. In fact, when we're most truthful we admit that illness wears us down; many of us can't even pray then. I suspect that when the Church speaks of praying for the sick it is not only for healing but on their behalf, in their stead as well. Both aspects of praying are possible in families. When I am not feeling well—low energy, worrisome symptoms, sleepless nights—I look to my husband or a child or a friend to pray for me, not necessarily for the dis-ease to go away, but simply to pray for me, whatever that means to them at the time.

The special events in the lives of family members, those events that call for celebration, are natural occasions for family prayer. Birthdays bring forth prayer of thanksgiving for that person's life. Graduations, the success of a project, a play or a concert—all can include a pause in the celebration for the family as community to acknowledge the source of all its growth and achievement and joy.

Special events that call for family prayer may be occasions of disappointment or sorrow. The loss of a job, the long awaited promotion that goes to another, misunderstanding, rejection—these, too, are special events in the lives of Christians. Some of our holiest days center around the disappointment, betrayal, suffering and death of the one we call Lord.

The sacraments are one form of common prayer in the lives of all Christian families. The first document to issue forth from the fathers of the Second Vatican Council declared what the monasteries had long known, that liturgy is at the heart of the Church's spiritual life and therefore at the heart of all our lives. But in the Constitution on the Sacred Liturgy the bishops caution that the full effects of worship are not automatic. The people must come to the Eucharist and to the other sacraments prepared and open to the moment. The celebrants, too, must recognize that their responsibility goes beyond mere observance of the law.

Eucharist is the most usual and the most constant way of community spiritual formation for families. It is the place of most intimate prayer, in a full and communal way, and a place for the family to experience what Evelyn Underhill calls the objective, unpossessive delight of worship.

Unfortunately, the parish often does not always reflect the spirit of the Constitution on the Sacred Liturgy, nor convey the power we know is possible in communal worship.[5] A family, parents especially, face a dilemma of discernment. Should they go elsewhere—perhaps to a college chapel—for worship, at least sometimes? Should they join another parish or a basic Christian community, if they can find one? Or simply persevere? I think many parents and teenagers face these and similar questions. Sometimes they lead to additional avenues of growth. I remember a conversation with one of my sons—now a student at a religious college—about his feeling "bored" at Mass. He was suggesting he no longer accompany us to Mass because only his body was there; his mind was elsewhere. There were two conversations, really. One was about liturgy, and my hope that he wouldn't make a judgment about whether to continue the practice of Sunday Mass until he had experienced the worship with a smaller group at the college he would be attending. That seemed reasonable to him. The second conversation was about boredom. Hesitatingly, I offered that it was important for a person to experience boredom. I did not lecture on the psychological and spiritual ramifications of boredom. Instead, we talked about people who are confined: the elderly, the chronically ill, the imprisoned. He listened. I know he is thinking about those people. I do not know if he is going to Mass, and I am not going to ask him. I think he will let me know, however.

The Sacrament of Reconciliation is another source of spiritual growth in families. I suspect it is underappreciated in our time, but I may be misreading the short confessional lines. If there is one central spiritual dynamic in family life, I suggest it is that of forgiveness. The Sacrament of Reconciliation celebrates that fact, and also helps to name those obstacles to forgiveness within ourselves. Of course, confession and forgiveness go on continually within the family. The sacramental celebration underscores that which is there daily in our lives.

In recent years the celebration of Eucharist in homes has meant a great deal to families, friends, and neighborhoods. When a friend of ours, a widow with ten grown children, entered the convent, those of us who knew her as friend and mentor wanted to say goodbye in a way that would be especially meaningful to her. We decided on a home Mass. This woman had sensitized many of us to the liturgical reforms of the Council and to the possibilities in home worship, so it seemed a fitting way to be with her then. It was a wonderful evening of celebration, and it recalled my memories of other home Masses: my son's First Communion, a Christmas Mass at our dining-room table after my husband's heart attack, a friend's wedding anniversary, a welcome Mass for new neighbors. Home Mass is not a frequent occurrence in our family's worship. But it is important when it happens. As the parish liturgy can bring the breadth of Christ to one's sense of Christian community, so a home Mass can open one to the depth and intimacy of Christ in the worshipping community.

The Rosary: The People's Prayer

Who knows how many generations of Catholic families have had as their common prayer the family rosary? There are many tales of families kneeling together in the living room or the sun porch with mother and father intoning Our Fathers and Hail Marys and children poking each other, tumbling to the floor, or falling asleep. My missionary friends in Latin America tell a different tale. They tell of families from generation to generation saying a nightly rosary with great seriousness; they tell, too, of gatherings of men and women and children joined by the rosary, a sign of solidarity with each other in the face of their poverty and oppression. For the Latins, Mary, Our Lady of Guadalupe, has been a symbol of liberation. She appeared to a poor illiterate layman—just like them—and the powerful Church authorities complied with her request to build a chapel, a request presented to the authorities by this poor man of the people. This remains a sign of hope to the people, and a woman is part of that hope for liberation.

The truth is that the rosary has appealed in every age and in every culture, adapted and enhanced according to circumstances. There is a transcendent steadfastness to it, despite the reservations of some theologians who probably have memories of long recitations in cold chapels. Nonetheless, I think we can properly call the rosary "the people's prayer."

Today there are probably few American or European households where the rosary is said together as family prayer. But, true to its history, it is a prayer for our time among some interesting groups and for different reasons. In some Christian feminist groups, a prayer in which a woman is recognized by the Church as central in salvation history is valued. The mysteries of the rosary, the meditation scenes, often feature Mary, thus meeting many women's need for feminine identification. One feminist I know told me that she feels strengthened every time she meditates on the fifth glorious mystery, the Coronation of Our Lady as Queen of Heaven. Another woman related how she began to say the rosary again after many years of not doing so: on a visit to Europe she saw painting after painting of Jesus crowning Mary, both of them seated. In these artistic-mystic images she saw intimations of the equality between man and woman.

Teenagers also value the rosary. There is something in the adolescent psyche that needs repetition, and needs also a present but distant mother. I am told by members of lay movements that attract youth—the Focolare and Taize, for example—that the rosary is a most appealing prayer. This is not hard to understand when you think about the repetitive rhythms of the music that appeals to this age group. In addition to whatever else it does, repetition also has the effect of calming the emotions. For young people this alone can provide moments of needed rest. The rosary is also a readily available prayer in times of stress of all kinds. Some years ago my daughter, then sixteen years old, was hit by a motorcycle as she was crossing the street. Her sister and a friend were with her. When the accident occurred, her sister raced to phone me at home and my husband at his office. When the ambulance arrived my daughter and her friend were saying the rosary aloud, much to the embarrassment of her sister, who reported the prayer episode to me when we all finally met at the hospital. When the immediate crisis was over, my injured daughter told me that she always says the rosary when she is frightened.

Meditators are yet another group. In the last twenty-five years methods of imaginative prayer, visualizations, mantras, and the like have been introduced to people of many religious traditions. Ordinary Catholic lay people who had little experience with meditation have discovered the riches in Saint Teresa's way and in the meditative way of Saint Ignatius. These are no longer well-kept secrets. This new generation of Christian meditators is applying its learning to the rosary. The recitation of the set prayers often achieves the same effect as a mantra, and the mysteries of the rosary are settings for meditative imagery.

I have prayed for my children in many ways, not always knowing why I chose this way or that. Now, in mid-life, I have more or less settled down to rosary praying for my family. Why? I feel right about the bonding with Mary. The repetition slows down my high-powered life. I can insert each child—now young men and women—into the various Gospel scenes and let them go. The beads are something physical to hold on to, important right now when my inner world feels more and more like an ocean.

When I was younger I tried and tried to pray the rosary; every one said I should, but I could not. Perhaps it was not my time. Now it is.

Prayer Alone

Following Jesus' pattern and the monks' ways, private prayer is certainly appropriate, even needed, in modern Christian families. Hidden prayer is a way of showing our love for others. One definition of love is that of giving our time and energy to another for the other's good. Intercessory prayer can be thought of in this way as spending time and personal energy on the others who are with us in family and on distant others whom we recognize as with us in God's family. Because intercessory prayer is a kind of nonmanipulative, noncontrolling way of loving, it represents one of the gifts of freedom we can give one another. This kind of prayer does not seek specific solutions, especially "my" solutions to a problem. Rather, it holds the person before God in an act of faith and trust in God, and an act of love for the person. It involves letting go of concrete expectations that can be yet another means of controlling the people in our lives.

Praying for one's children is an exercise of parental ministry. In some mysterious way it creates spiritual bonds between parent and child while at the same time acknowledging that this child is created in God's image, not mine.

Pray Always

Saint Paul told the Thessalonians that they should pray constantly and that they should give thanks in all circumstances (1 Thess. 5:17–18). Ever since, Christians have been pondering what he meant. But even in the wondering there is a general assent that prayer is the very pulse of the spiritual life, essential for all vocations. It is the food of Christian family spirituality just as it is the primary nourishment in monastic families. Common prayer and private prayer intersect all the pathways of ordinary family life. Prayer is a place of unfolding *intimacy* and helps us to grow closer to those who share life with us. To be together before God, in silence or with words, is to share some sacred time and space. Prayer is an instrument of *egalitarianism* because before God we know we are equal. This strengthens the bonds of our human and Christian solidarity. To pray is to experience ourselves under the *authority* of Christ and, as such, is a means of examining the place of authority in our daily living. Do we avoid authority, or abuse it? To whom and for whom are we responsible? Such questions are put to us in prayer. Prayer opens us to the depth of wisdom. It teaches us. We *study* in prayer: ourselves, others, God, and we are impelled to new learning, to new creative challenges. In prayer we relax and, like children, enjoy being with God. In this way, prayer is like *play.* We return to work and study and responsibilities refreshed. All our temptations to flee from our people, from our work, from love, from ourselves, can rise during times of prayer and we can see them undisguised, name them and confess them, and so strengthen our commitment to *stability.* Prayer beckons us to trust the absolute darkness of *solitude,* and thereby to learn really to see the world we inhabit and those who inhabit it with us. We can see children, spouse, friends, no longer as extensions of ourselves but as themselves. Because prayer carves out more and more room for God, our capacity to receive others, all of whom are in God, is enlarged. Prayer changes us. We become increasingly *hospitable.* A day comes when we find ourselves saying "not please, but thank you," as Annie Dillard simply and eloquently noted in *Pilgrim at Tinker Creek.* Then the praise of our Creator springs up in our hearts and is on our lips. We are praying always. The inner self is coming of age.

Chapter 5

SOLITUDE

In the morning, long before dawn, he got up and left the
house, and went off to a lonely place and prayed there.

Mark 1:35

Monasticism, growing as it did out of the desert experience of
withdrawal and aloneless, has retained throughout its history a
respectful guardianship over silence and solitude. In fact, silence is one of the three capital virtues of the monk mentioned
in the Rule of Benedict, the other two being humility and obedi-
ence.

The structures of monastic community life allowed for silence
and solitude in the rhythm of each day. A certain number of
hours were to be devoted daily to *lectio,* which included reading,
private prayer and meditation, and the memorization of and
rumination on biblical texts. In this way the monk's mind was
to be filled constantly with the Word of God, and that experience helped shape the whole of his inner psychology.[1] The
scholarship and learning for which the monasteries of Europe
were justly famous also happened in an atmosphere of quiet,
with little interruption and with the opportunity to work alone.

Unnecessary talk or idle chatter was discouraged. Silence was
considered a "watchful guardian over sinful talk" and a necessary prerequisite for listening to the Spirit. Monks were told that
they should diligently cultivate silence at all times, but espe-

cially at night. After Compline, the final night prayer of the Church, *total* silence characterized the monastery.

Why the emphasis on solitude and especially silence? The Commentary on the Rule provides a clue: "The silence and relative solitude maintained by reducing contact with the world outside to a minimum created an atmosphere that favored recollection."[2] Does the monastic value of silence and solitude have any relevance today especially for modern families? How is it related to the spiritual life and growth of the twentieth-century person?

Life and Solitude

Many years ago, amid the chaos, confusion, and din of Nazi Germany, Max Picard wrote movingly about the power of silence in a person's life. Silence is a basic phenomenon, he wrote, and when one stands before a basic phenomenon, one is confronted by the beginning of all things.[3] The same thing could be said about solitude, I think, because it belongs to that radical kind of aloneness that has long been recognized as a necessary prelude to and context for creativity of all kinds. Obviously, painters and composers and writers and weavers must do their work alone. But even before the paint is laid on the canvas or threads are bound together, the creator has surely experienced solitude, periods of still waiting, of being prepared, perhaps by God, for some outward expression of one's inner world.

Life grows in and out of stark solitude. This is something farmers know when they plant seeds that will remain for months in darkness, unseen. This is something that parents know, too, as they wait for the birth of a child, who develops in secret, deep within the mother's body. This is something that each man and woman knows who is growing in consciousness of his or her being. One *knows* that personal giftedness, if it is to grow strong, requires a certain amount of respectful privacy.

If we are to create ourselves, to become artful human beings in our marriages and in our various family settings, to become conscious of our lives as connected to God's ongoing creativity, solitude must surely have some place. Why? What happens in the lonely, unseen places?

Alone and apart one is able to rest from the continual stimulation of interpersonal relations, of expectations, of evaluating life projects. There is rest from the alertness necessary to keep our households and work places functioning. Furthermore, research into experiences of extended solitude shows that here one inevitably confronts the ultimate questions of life and death, of meaning and suffering. This is as true of prisoners or the chronically ill or the handicapped as it is of those who voluntarily enter into extended solitude. The latter category includes mystics and religious personalities as well as artists and scientists and social reformers. Catherine of Siena, for example, spent three years in her room, secluded from her family and the ordinary life of medieval Italy. There, alone, she developed her capacity for deep communion with God before embarking on a future of intense political and religious activity throughout the Italian city-states. Our history is filled with such stories: Ignatius and Benedict are two examples. Florence Nightingale used a period of sickness and confinement to gain clarity about the totality of her nursing vocation. Her solitude, unlike that of Catherine, Ignatius, and Benedict, was not freely chosen, but was nonetheless fruitful.

Periods of regular solitude interspersed in the daily, weekly, and monthly activities of ordinary twentieth-century women and men still lead to confrontation with fundamental life questions, and to conviction about action, as well as opening us to genuine rest. It will probably happen more slowly and less intensely than, say, in the life of Catherine of Siena, as the accretions of a cluttered life are scraped away bit by bit, to reveal interior spaciousness. But it will happen.

Obstacles to Solitude

How strange, then, that, although solitude is yearned for, and its importance recognized, it looms for so many as an unattainable goal or as a luxury in an era filled with the miracles of technology. No doubt there is something here of Saint Paul's insight that we fail to carry out the things we want to do and find ourselves doing the very things we hate (Rom. 7). But there are also social factors that affect all of life and influence the choices we make. Urbanization is one factor: more families live now in cities, where there is less physical space than in rural settings. Contemporary architecture is another factor: houses constructed after World War II feature great open family rooms, with kitchen and living space and dining area all blending into each other. Small secluded studies, libraries, or music rooms belong to homes of another era. Consequently, it is sometimes difficult if not impossible to locate what Virginia Woolf termed a room of one's own, a place sacred for one's solitude.

A more pervasive and subtle obstacle, one more difficult to circumvent, is the cultural milieu that values producing and achieving and is suspicious of wasting time, which is often what true solitude looks like. Many people are simply afraid to be alone. "Loneliness is such an omnipotent and painful threat to many persons that they have little conception of the positive values of solitude. . . . In our culture it is permissible to say you are lonely, for that is a way of admitting that it is good to be alone. And it is permissible to want to be alone temporarily, 'to get away from it all.' But if one mentioned at a party that he likes to be alone, not for a rest or an escape but for its own joy, people would think that something was vaguely wrong with him. . . . It is inconceivable to them that he would choose to be alone."[4]

To structure solitude into one's life is to be, to some extent, countercultural. It helps to remember that Christian life, while always exchanging with the culture in which it is embedded at a given time, has maintained its right and duty to critique the same culture, to be, as it were, a counterpoint, demonstrating alternative ways of being in life. Historically, monasteries have offered radical alternatives to the predominant culture.

Christian communities can speak from historical authenticity on this subject and can therefore help the men and women of our time move through these obstacles to a reconstruction of life patterns where solitude can find a place in marriage and family life, as in the domestic churches spoken about by Pope Paul VI.[5]

Solitude and Marriage

A two-person covenantal group is the smallest form of family. In the Christian tradition, marriage is a vowed and sacramental covenant between a man and a woman, the unique expression of family and at the same time the most common. Husband and wife, while still individual persons, become one, and Saint Paul tells us that this is a sign of Christ's unity with the Church. The participation of husband and wife in creativity is also unique (and also common), because it has the potential for creating human life, giving birth to persons, nurturing them and enabling them to grow to maturity and to begin again the cycle of birth and life. But this oneness does not mean that all differences collapse. Nor does it mean that marital creativity excludes personal and individual creative expression.

One does not often hear of the value of solitude for a creative marriage. On the contrary, the Christian churches in recent years have increasingly emphasized aspects of marital "being together." Such things as couple prayer, joint Scripture reading, partner apostolates, and other joint ventures have been prominent in discussions on Christian marriage. Many married people affirm that these gestures of unity have strengthened the marriage covenant in the face of little or no societal support for marriage, at least in the Western countries. But it is, I suggest, a partial understanding of unity, and certain questions occur.

Are these particular outward signs of unity equated with the inner bond? Has the fundamental value of solitude been forgotten in the efforts to "make a couple"?

Not long ago, when my daughter was married, the presiding priest spoke of marriage as a work of art. He said that marriage, like sculpture or painting or dance, requires patience, vision, willingness to begin again. I mentally added: and a respect for solitude. I recalled a letter of Rainer Maria Rilke in which he said that someday the love-experience would be reshaped into that of one human being to another; personhood would be central. He wrote:

> And this more human love (that will fulfill itself, infinitely considerate and gentle, and kind and clear in binding and releasing) will resemble that which we are preparing with struggle and toil, the love that consists in this, that two solitudes protect and border and salute each other.[6]

John Dunne argues that all persons committed to the inward journey come to realize the truth that we cannot live without conflict and suffering, that we cannot avoid guilt, that we must someday die, and that in all these things we are alone and cannot make one another unalone.[7] This is true, I believe, even for husband and wife. The Christian community in the person of significant others can be with us, but the experiential reality is surely ours alone.

Undoubtedly, some men and women choose marriage to escape from this radical aloneness, the primordial experience that each person bears in the depths of his or her being. When escape is found to be impossible and when increased interaction and distraction, including endless discussions and "giving to others," fail to achieve the idealized unity, then the marriage is perceived to be a failure. But perhaps the real failure is the failure to recognize and honor the basic human need for solitude, in oneself and in the other, and to help each other locate, figuratively and literally, the Gospel's lonely place.

Many women, particularly in recent years, have felt themselves collapsing under the weight of expectations that they will care for husband, home, children, community, school, social life—and perhaps careers—all in some perfected, generous, selfless way. They have sought space and rest in the only way that seemed feasible: leave-taking. I wonder how many women would feel compelled to distance themselves so drastically from their families if community norms, including those in the church community, recognized their rights and those of other family members to privacy and uninterrupted solitude on a regular basis.

Sometimes women—and men, for that matter—who want to separate for a time from family life are asking simply to go apart awhile and rest. They are not necessarily seeking the rupture of the relationship, but rather healing. All schools of wisdom know that rest is a necessary component of healing. With the realization that this is an authentic human rhythm, perhaps more marriages could be strengthened and preserved for continued common life.

Recently a woman in her early forties came to talk with me about some inner conflict she was experiencing. Her marriage of eighteen years was severely strained. She and her husband had been through many years of therapy and marriage counseling, alone and together. She was at the point of wanting a divorce, of simply not wanting to struggle anymore. Confused feelings surfaced when she was at Mass. There, her marriage vows, her commitment before God, dominated her thoughts. She translated her inability to be happy in the marriage and her lack of confidence in therapy as unwillingness. At Mass she thought, "If only I try harder, things will get better." But things were only getting worse, and her guilt grew.

As we talked I could feel her exhaustion. I suggested that maybe she needed to go away for a while to rest from the unceasing effort at togetherness, and that she might use the period of extended solitude as an opportunity to begin in earnest her own spiritual journey. She was both surprised and relieved to think that there was the possibility of spiritual discovery and wholeness for her in ways other than working directly on the marriage *at this time.* Separation for spiritual search is a qualitatively different experience than divorce.

I do not know if this particular marriage will survive. I believe, however, that the experience of solitude will help this woman assess her own inner resources and her inner freedom, thus enabling her to choose or not to choose to remain in the marriage from a point of integrity rather than from anger. There is a danger that she will fill her newfound space with new stimulation and new emotional ties and thus evade the risk of journeying, for a while at least, alone and unencumbered. She will need considerable courage in the face of a culture that warns, "Don't be alone; it is dangerous."

The Family and Solitude

Modern family life is very complex. Children's and parents' schedules weave tightly in and out of each other. Time unaccounted for is rare. How then does one carve out some solitude?

First of all, people generally manage to do what they want to do; to want time alone is the beginning of solitude. Second, one needs to look at the particular configuration of one's own family: the responsibilities particular people acknowledge toward each other, the needs of the family members, their ages and health. How solitude happens will depend largely on the conditions within each family. For example, working mothers and fathers of preschool or school-age children may have the most difficulty in allowing themselves to take some regular blocks of time to do nothing that is readily visible or measurable. When time is taken from the workplace the natural inclination is to spend that time with one's children. Working mothers particularly tend to feel guilty for not being at home when their children return from school. An occasional day off, therefore, is usually given to the children. This attitude is understandable and reflects the need to structure time with one's children into the family's way of life, but not as a substitute for solitude.

Some working parents find that they are more rested—ultimately—if they rise early in the morning to allow thirty, forty, or sixty minutes of quiet time alone before the day's activities get underway. In addition, parents of a growing energetic family often discover they really need more time than that. They need to mark on the calendar and claim in their lives one or two mornings a month to be alone, away from the ever-present need to achieve. I have known fathers and mothers who have taken leave time for this purpose, and they attest to its restorative and re-creative value.

Since solitude is not generally valued by organizations or secular communities, difficulties can arise if employers are unwilling to grant employees time off on a regular basis. This needs to be talked about openly and the value of solitude explained. On the other hand, women and men in executive positions may find the greatest difficulty in themselves, in their reluctance to let go of high-powered decision making for even a short while. In all cases, the conviction that solitude is of value, not only for family life but also for one's professional life, can help to release both men and women from the tyranny of constant presence on the job.

Mothers at home every day with young children have to search for possibilities for alone time. When I was a young mother with a household of four preschool children, with community and church responsibilities and with guests from time to time, all my innermost instincts pointed toward the need for regular solitude and silence, for the experience of quiet prayer, of listening to God. How was this to be done?

Several years ago I wrote about this situation in *The Wind Is Rising*:

I looked at the shape of a typical day and noticed some space. There was nap time, usually grasped at as an opportunity to accomplish tasks I couldn't get to while the children were awake. Instead of stuffing the space of nap time with various good deeds, I stopped and did nothing . . . or so it seemed. No radio, no telephone, just silence. I entered this mid-day sabbath, sometimes with Scripture, sometimes with other writings, often with restlessness and anxiety, sometimes with eager anticipation, and frequently with fatigue. My time alone often ended in sleep, just like the children.[8]

I look back on those afternoons as some of the more important moments in my entire life. The steadiness of solitude and silence was a kind of formation process, the effects of which I still bear within me.

Just as husband and wife, mother and father, need to find and honor time apart from each other and the children, they also need to be alone together. This represents time and space where they are simply with each other, without the distraction of home duties, parental responsibilities, or outside stimulation. Solitude together means a turning toward each other, or a being side by side, inhabiting together some private space. This is closely allied to intimacy. Because home is more than likely filled with the emotional vibrations of daily life, it may be necessary to live these blocks of solitude away. This might mean a semiannual or annual retreat together. It might involve a trip to the country, or it might be as simple as a walk in the city park or a weekly luncheon date for the sole purpose of talking with each other uninterruptedly, an unusual happening for parents in the center of a busy household. Whatever form this alone time together takes, it must be honored, just as personal solitude must. Unclaimed, it slips away.

Children need privacy as well as parents. If the creative seeds in each child are to grow and flourish, they must be nurtured in places of privileged privacy. This becomes especially subtle in adolescence, the tender time of life when both distance and intimacy are necessary. Too much privacy and distance from the family may signal trouble. And yet the growing personality needs to grow apart in order to grow up into an autonomous person. As in all other things, balance is crucial. The experience of solitude in the parents' own lives will help them to be discerners, to see what their adolescent children really are saying by their absence. Is it alienation? Or is it that sacred time of rest and restoration?

It should not be forgotten that the family community— whether it be a single parent and children, young parents and a baby, a household of young adults, a multigenerational family —needs to step back from its continuing encounter with the larger world. It needs to pause for a while and reestablish its identity as a family. Just as solitude confirms autonomy for individual persons, it confirms the solidarity of the members as *this* family as belonging to each other and accountable to each other. Communal solitude may be as ordinary as a "sacred Sunday brunch," or as special as an annual family retreat. What is important is that life is arranged so that family members may encounter one another in an environment free from external intrusions. It is here that they can really see each other as the support and challenge they are to each other.

In the Solitude

Questions and concerns inevitably arise about *what to do* in the solitude, whether it be individual alone time, or alone time with others. It is natural to wonder how one undertakes the solitary pilgrimage.

The surprising thing about solitude is the eventual discovery that one is not lonely, but instead that new dimensions of our communitarian nature emerge. Solitude gently leads one into contemplation where the Other awaits.

May Sarton describes a moment of shared solitude that somewhat answers the questions about what happens. She and a friend have shared a picnic by a waterfall. She writes in her journal:

> And then the silence fell.
> We simply sat there and drank in the dappled water, a couple of gulls swimming around a big rock, and far away a pine-covered island and beyond that rising up in the distance the deep blue rounded peaks of the Sandwich range. How rare in our world to sit absolutely still for an hour, not thinking, not even feeling, simply being in the presence of great beauty. At first one notices the small things, the subtle changes as wind suddenly ruffles a small space in the water, the amber color of still water over sand, or the reflection of a single tree, but little by little, it is the whole unified scene that takes over. And it is silence itself that unifies it. One slides down deep, deep into contemplation. This is not ecstasy like the light on lavendar petals. It is more like prayer. Beauty beyond our understanding and beyond our uniqueness as individuals. Presence that asks nothing of us except to be in its presence.[9]

Not all periods of solitude will ensure such a unitive experience, but the practice of attentiveness and observation will certainly predispose one to such moments.

Regular time alone helps to develop and expand the contemplative capacity, particularly as we practice attentiveness. Sometimes this means unlearning the scattered way of trying to be attentive to many things all at once. Concentration can be learned through the arts and through crafts. The potter's wheel, the weaver's loom, the canvas, the calligrapher's pen—these are the instruments of concentration that capture, hold, and direct one's energy to a particular point in the creative process. Behind that point is the Creator.

Crafts are not the only path to concentration. Evelyn Underhill teaches that practical mysticism can grow in a person from simply being present to the everyday, readily available contents of life. Walking, jogging, cooking, gardening, all offer the possibility of uncluttering one's mind and spirit. A rose, for example, can be the vehicle for a contemplative act. Looking with full attention at a rose, being with the rose, noting the shadings, the harmonious folds of petals, the rose's center, the texture, the scent; staying with the rose, uniting with it, moving beyond the rose to the source of all that one experiences there can bring one to the God who holds each rose and each person in existence.

All household tasks have the potential for expanding and deepening contemplative awareness. This explicitly active contemplation is an apt preparation for attentiveness to the unseen, to the quiet prayer and silent meditation that aligns us with God. As the taste for solitude grows, time will be found, even in the busiest schedules, for quiet, solitary prayer.

The East

One of the great ecumenical conversations of our time is that between Christian contemplatives and the wisdom of the Eastern non-Christian religions. Although the Catholic Church has been a guardian and preserver of a cherished contemplative tradition, it has sometimes guarded that heritage so well that the ways of contemplative prayer have not been widely available. The buried treasure has had to be hunted. Thomas Keating believes the Reformation was a decisive factor in promoting the view that contemplation was something special for special people. For the first fifteen centuries, Father Keating says, the Church taught uninterruptedly that contemplation is a part of a genuine spiritual life and therefore open to all Christians, not just the cloistered or the religiously vowed. But from the time of the Reformation and the Counter-Reformation the sense that contemplation was a normal development in the spiritual life of ordinary people was lost.[10]

But now Christian women and men from all walks of life are again entering the world of immediate experience, where God is not so much thought about or believed in as known. And they have been helped by teachers from the East, and by Christians who have journeyed East to learn. Eastern wisdom and practice have been showing Western analytical Christians how to pay attention to their bodies, for example. The importance of breathing and posture and relaxation as a preliminary to natural contemplative prayer is no longer a secret.

The many young people who have tasted Zen and have returned to Christian prayer feel at home in the place of darkness and stillness, the "night of the Spirit," as John of the Cross called it. They are willing to wait there, asking nothing, seeking nothing, but open, waiting upon God. Their hours of *zazen* have taught them well.[11]

This imageless, wordless way of simple adoration is favored by feminists whose sensibilities can no longer relate to the predominantly masculine religious imagery in the Judeo-Christian prayer forms. These feminists include men as well as women.

There are other prayers of solitude and quiet. The prayer of centering has been retrieved from the fourteenth-century *Cloud of Unknowing* and now is available to ordinary men and women.[12] The Jesus Prayer combined with hatha-yoga is also practiced by quite a few Christians, and there are many more variations, I'm sure.

Probably there are not large crowds of Christians sitting daily in quiet contemplation, but there are some. Many of them are mothers, fathers, students, workers, religious, priests—people committed to solitary contemplation as part of their overall Christian devotion. Once again, monks who themselves are traveling this desert path and who recognize the markers along the way, are willing to be with others who are just venturing forth.

Scripture

One sign of Christian renewal is the comfort and delight that people now find in private reading of the Scriptures. No longer is there the fear of private interpretation. Men and women are learning to pray the Scriptures and have confidence in doing so.

One of the least-practiced scriptural prayer methods, however, is that direct inheritance from monasticism, *lectio divina.* Yet this is one of the more comprehensive meditative-contemplative-dialogic ways of prayer available to Christians. It is a prayer suited for solitude, and a way to move consciously in God through the activities of the day.[13]

Notations on Solitude

Because experience is so fluid and often so difficult to name, writing can be a helpful means of marking and mapping the spiritual journey, which is intensified in solitude. There are many methods of journal writing, and many Christians have engaged in one or another of them.

After trying different methods and learning from them, I seem to have settled into a straightforward routine of writing at the end of a period of solitude and prayer and also at the end of the day. Sometimes the writing is a stream of free associations; sometimes it is a written meditation on a central question in my life at a given moment; often it is a recounting of the story of the day. Always it is a way of owning my experience and of recognizing God in the solitary spaces of a given day.

Perhaps a good way for anyone to begin to structure solitude into life is to write about it: its availability; its absence; how one feels about it, positively and negatively; how it can come to be, and whether we want it to be.

Solitude and Community

There is a story told of two friends who attended an ongoing seminar conducted by the eminent twentieth-century psychologist Carl Jung. The friends left a particular meeting in silence and concentration, deeply touched by what had transpired. One said, "Today Dr. Jung has truly talked about myself and my crucial problems, and answered all my unasked questions." The other protested, "But no, he talked about my problem." More protestations. Finally they stopped, looked at each other and realized that what had happened was that a man had talked to them out of his own depths, from the most fundamental level of being, and in so doing included their individual personalities. More importantly, he transcended them.

This story is recounted by A. M. Allchin, who states that when we reach a certain depth of human life and experience, a certain depth of holiness, we find that our existence as persons is very different from our existence as individuals.[14]

The journey to the center of one's life does not leave a person isolated and alone. True solitude is rather a bridge to communion with other persons. We see this in the construct of the words themselves. Solitude means one, alone. Unity means the joining of many ones into one. (This is perhaps best expressed in the Russian language where the words for solitude, one, unity, and union are all derived from the same root word.) We see that solitude and "being with everyone" are very close indeed.

I mentioned this linguistic discovery to a friend who replied that unless a person has been able to concentrate on knowing himself or herself—and solitude is a condition for this knowledge—our seeking after self-knowledge will always intrude upon our being with and for others. He meant, I think, that until we have looked at and seen our own self we will be searching for this self in others. Then how will we ever see the other? And love the one who is different?

The ultimate communitarian nature of solitude and silence is described by one of Chaim Potok's characters, the son of a Hassidic rabbi and spiritual leader, a *tzaddik*. The boy speaks about his growing up in an atmosphere of silence.

My father himself never talked to me, except when we studied together. He taught me with silence. He taught me to look into myself, to find my own strength, to walk around inside myself in company with my soul. When his people would ask him why he was so silent with his son, he would say to them that he did not like to talk, words are cruel, words play tricks, they distort what is in the heart, they conceal the heart, the heart speaks through silence. One learns of the pain of others by suffering one's own pain, he would say, by turning inside oneself, by finding one's own soul. And it is important to know of pain, he said. It destroys our self-pride, our arrogance, our indifference toward others. It makes us aware of how frail and tiny we are and of how much we must depend upon the Master of the Universe. Only slowly, very slowly, did I begin to understand what he was saying. For years his silence bewildered and frightened me, though I always trusted him, I never hated him. And when I was old enough to understand, he told me that of all people a tzaddik especially must know of pain. A tzaddik must know how to suffer for his people, he said. He must take their pain from them and carry it on his own shoulders. He must carry it always. He must grow old before his years. He must cry, in his heart he must always cry. Even when he dances and sings, he must cry for the sufferings of his people.[15]

Not all of us are called to be spiritual leaders like the *tzaddik*, but we are called to be spiritual people. This includes some solitude and silence so that when we come into another's presence we can see the sacred contours and meet the other in trust.

Chapter 6

PLAY

Unless you become like little children you shall not enter the kingdom of heaven.

Matthew 18:3

I do not think of myself as a playful person. A typical day in my life includes prayer, reading, conversation, writing, meetings, meals, sleep. Sometimes there is shopping and entertaining. Sometimes I listen to music, or my husband reads aloud to me, or I to him. I have never thought of all this as play.

Many of my friends play tennis or swim everyday; I do not. I do not join my husband in jogging, a typical part of his day. I walk, just to walk, only on vacations or retreats. Chesspieces stand alert in my living room—ancient enemies, the Christians and the Moors—ready for a game I never play. Most of our children and my husband play bridge whenever they can, and if they need a fourth I might oblige; but I almost never initiate a game. I go to the theater whenever I can and to films when somebody suggests it. I never watch television and I play the piano about three times a year.

So, I was not too surprised when I presented the thesis for this book—that the monastic dynamics of ordinary living were a framework for experiencing God in family life—and a workshop participant noticed the absence of play in the model. But I thought it a revealing gap, and one worthy of investigation.

What I unearthed were some personal insights and some assumptions about monasticism.

It was true that I had missed play as a dynamic common to both monasticism and family life, although I was aware of the fact that recreation is part of the structure of religious communities. On a retreat once in a cloistered convent, I participated in the regular recreation period. There was talking and singing; some sisters embroidered. Essentially it was a group activity. We began and ended the recreation together. When the alloted time was over, I went to my room and the sisters dispersed. Like many people I know, the sisters count play as important to their human and spiritual growth.

It seemed clear that play had to be part of this book, but I dreaded it. Yet, once it was a chapter in my mind, a committed part of the book's structure, the associations around play and the possibilities in it began to skip around the edges of my consciousness.

My investigation yielded several discoveries. First, I found nothing about play or recreation in the Rule of Benedict and nothing in the commentaries I consulted. Why, I wondered? I realize the Rule is not a definitive blueprint for all forms of Christian communitarian life; it is more a summary of the monastic tradition that preceded Benedict. So it is brief and elastic. Commentators agree that Benedict did not intend his Rule for all monks always and everywhere, but for his own community. He handed on to his own family what he had learned from his experience. And his experience, or at least the experience of his own culture, may have impelled him to exclude play or recreation from the monastic life he was ordering. The connotations of play during the decline of the Roman Empire were probably not inspirational for Christian community life. However, the traditions upon which Saint Benedict drew, the Fathers of the Church and the wisdom of ancient Rome and Greece, offer many observations about play.

My second discovery was that my notion of play had, for a

long time, been narrowly defined. The more I investigated the more I realized that play is present in my life.

There is a third discovery: I want to play even more.

The Wisdom of the Church and Play

The concept of play appears in the Scriptures, both Old and New Testaments; in the writings of the patristic period, and in the works of mystics and saints as a form of participation, in the deepest sense, in the life of God. Jesus himself tells us that unless we are like little children we shall not enter the Kingdom. A usual interpretation of this saying is that children trust their parents and, like them, we must trust God. Quite true. But is that all? Observe the little children in their homes, on the streets, in day-care centers, little children too young for competitive school sports and after school activities. What do children do? They play. They play with an intense seriousness. They are *in* their play. They lose themselves there. For them, play is their work. I believe that this was Maria Montessori's penetrating insight about the nature of early childhood.

All parents have watched their children build castles of blocks or sand, intent on their play-work, absorbed in the act of creating. Then, an ocean wave breaks upon the shore, or a big brother or sister walks by, and the castle is no more. There are tears over the destruction, but they are only temporary. The child possesses a detachment, and tomorrow he will once again be building castles, or maybe tunnels. The child's imagination is not attached to the results. It is open, and all things are possible.

Hugo Rahner, in a splendid short study,[1] presents a medley of sayings from ancient philosophy and the patristic period to support the contention that the human person should imitate God at play, that is, God's own creative power, by a lightness of touch, regard for beauty, by wisdom, and by the sober seriousness of the endeavor.[2] Rahner's playful person is a "grave-merry one." Laughter and tears are close companions, as we see they are with our own children.

Apparently the monks of the primitive Church had quite a bit to say on the subject of play, even if it does not appear in the Rule of Benedict or its predecessors. Augustine, for example, wrote that "the truly wise man will now and then relax the tension of his mind and let its sharp edge be dulled."[3] And in Rahner's opinion, the early Fathers wrote their loveliest pages around the theme of our earthly life as a divine children's game. In Jerome, for example, we read, "O City of God . . . in her the joy of the Spirit finds expression in a bodily gesture, and her children shall say with David as they dance the solemn step, 'I will dance and play before the face of the Lord.' "[4] Dancing and playing are central in Rahner's reflections. "All play has somewhere deep within it an element of the dance; it is a kind of dance round the truth."[5]

Rahner tells us how some of the saints viewed play, and his telling forms a delightful mosaic. Mechthild of Magdeburg speaks about the divine resolve that the human race should be redeemed: "Then the Holy Ghost made play for the Father with great gentleness . . . and said, 'Lord, dear Father, we would no longer be unfruitful.' "[6] And Teresa of Lisieux expresses her desire to be nothing more than a toy, a little ball for the child Jesus, "a toy of no value—a ball say—such as a child might throw on the ground or leave lying in a corner or press to his heart if he feels that way about it."[7] She is talking about the play of grace, the worthiness of God, the sure sense that after all is done, all that can be said in truth is that we are unprofitable servants (Luke 17:10).

The fact that God put on human flesh, uniting mind, body, and spirit, and the fact that the Church has always celebrated this in some form of bodily gesture, leads Rahner to a kind of restrained plea for dance—in our lives? in the Church? perhaps both? He is not definitive in this. He recognizes that music and dance played no liturgical role in the ancient Church, understandably, since Christianity of early times was distancing itself from pagan expressions of religious spirit.[8] The Puritans extended this distancing to the point of total prohibition. Nevertheless, Rahner finds that dance (play) still has been expressed in almost every century and in every culture. God cannot be contained. "Dance really signifies a high tension of joy . . . for it is a rhythmical motion of the body in which the inner disposition of the soul is made visible to the bodily eye; for man is of a dual nature and consists both of body and soul."[9]

The wisdom of antiquity, the Scriptures, the Fathers of the Church, the saints and mystics of the Christian faith have led Rahner to ask a poignant and exciting question for our time:

> How can a religious man express the nature of what he hopes for in the life to come save through the inadequate medium of visual images and words? He hopes for freedom, rest, release from all preoccupations of mind, for untroubled gladness of soul; he longs to be once more a child, a child in utter security, and like a child, to play; he hopes, in a word, for that complete heart's ease that will allow even his body, freed now from the burden of its earthly life, to move and sway to the meaning of the heavenly dance.[10]

Can We Dance Today?

Can Rahner's question begin to be answered on this side of life? Perhaps. Last year a hundred people from all over the United States gathered for a national conference on American spirituality. They were mostly lay people, family people, working people. There were some priests and sisters, too, and seven bishops and a Cistercian abbot. One of the liturgies was a Gospel Mass, emphasizing African-Catholic ritual. The Mass began with a choir processing in a stylized Ethiopian march; behind the choir came the bishops and the abbot caught up in the spirit of the celebration and concentrating all their energy on the structured yet freeing dance step. They were as intent as children at play. The congregation also became intent as we watched them. We were *in* the worship, body and soul.

Throughout that three-day conference we paid attention to our bodies. Some people rose at 6:30 A.M. for an hour of yoga and *tai-chi.* Workshops in prayer and sculpture, drawing, and dance offered physical ways of being present to God, opening up some untried ways into contemplation. And there was movement—body prayer—in the form of evening-prayer gestures and eucharistic praise. We found that by attending to our bodies during worship we were more concentrated and more present.

This conference enabled us to see and experience the various ways that connections are being made in our time between the spiritual journey and play.[11] Experiences such as this spirituality conference are helping more and more Christians realize how out of touch most of us are with our bodies and how important it is to get back in touch. In the United States and in the northern European countries most people no longer have the benefits of an agrarian culture or of regular manual labor. In the absence of natural body awareness, exercise and sports are intentionally included in many daily schedules. For example, a friend of mine rises every weekday morning at five o'clock for several hours of tennis and running before the start of the day's other activities. He considers this daily ritual of physical exercise as necessary to his life as food. He says that not only is his body refreshed but his mind is cleansed and he is centered for his day of work. Clearly, not everyone finds tennis such an integrating experience. But my friend does represent, I think, one aspect of contemporary spirituality, namely, awareness of life through awareness of the body.

Kathryn Fredgren is one who has commited her whole life to building awareness that our bodies are temples of God's Holy Spirit. She is a professional dancer, a performer and now a teacher. She is also a mother. For her, dance is not at all limited to studio or stage; rather it has expanded into a ministry wherein she helps people become aware that "God is alive in us." She speaks of the body with great reverence. "Our bodies are our beings," she says, "they are our instruments of ministry." Everybody can dance, she's convinced, because dance is simply the body reacting to the environment. Her classes in movement begin with awakening the participants to their bodies in very simple and gentle ways: "Observe the people around you," she recommends to her beginning students. In careful observation she knows that we can see what others are saying and feeling. Are they bowed down? Lonely? Scared? Apathetic? Sad? It is all there in the body. When you know how others feel, reach out to them, touch them physically, she adds. She agrees that families are the first and most natural places for this observation and touching. Although Kathryn believes that touching is our most desired experience, she says it is also the most feared. You get past the fear a little at a time.

She asks her students to study their hands, to meditate on all that has passed through them, all that they have held in a day, all that they have pushed away. Hands are instruments of ministry, she maintains. Once the hands and touching are appreciated, one can build respect for the whole body; the next step is to enjoy it, and then to celebrate it—let it dance, wherever it may be.

As Kathryn talked, I recalled my young Parisian friend Martine. Not long ago we were together in the Rodin Museum, feeling the power of the bodies sculpted in marble and metal. We talked about the human body. I told her that I thought feet were truly wonderful because they connect us to the earth, the same earth that has been walked upon by Cicero and Caesar, by Shakespeare and Rodin, by Jesus and us. Martine agreed, but said that hands connect us to each other directly. We reach out and become one with others by means of hands. I think we agreed that in the dance, hands *and* feet together express the emotional and spiritual energy of the person.

The Many Forms of Dance

If we think of dance analogically, beyond the conventional definitions and forms, if we think of it in terms of "inner dance" or unself-conscious presence, or if we think of it as delight in being, either alone or with others, then we see that there may be more play within our family group than we thought. I, for one, have found this to be true.

When my children were small I played with them, or more properly stated, I let them play with me. We cooked together and cleaned together. We gardened. For me, work is often my play and I invited the children to join me in my play. They made little loaves of bread and huge gingerbread men. With small pans of soapy water they scrubbed furniture. They dug small gardens and often ate their half-grown vegetables. I read to them and played the piano for them. In a way, I played with them the games I knew.

There were other occasions for play: vacations, for instance. We usually vacationed in the summer in a secluded cabin without television, radio, or telephone. There we sailed and swam and fished and looked. We all remember those times as non-achievement periods, except for the competition of evening Monopoly games. We read together, sharing silence in the common reading room. It was during these summer vacations that we taught the children to play bridge, a game which still gives them an opportunity to play together as young adults.

There is a dance that is special to marriage. In Genesis there is a wonderful story about Isaac and Rebecca. During a time of famine they wander into Philistine territory in search of food. When the people ask Isaac about his wife, he answers that Rebecca is his sister. We are told that he gave this reply because Rebecca was beautiful and Isaac was afraid the Philistines would kill him in order to take Rebecca. His story was believed and they remained in the land for quite some time. But one day the king looked out his window and saw Isaac fondling Rebecca and he knew that something was wrong with Isaac's story (Gen. 26:9). (Some versions of this narrative say Isaac was playing with Rebecca.) The king summoned Isaac and said to him, "Surely she must be your wife." Well, Isaac owned up to the real relationship, and all was well. But the point is that husbands and wives do indeed play with each other. They look at each other, with eyes meeting eyes, "a look into a look," as Walker Percy's Allison put it.[12] They touch each other, embrace, and laugh, not only as preliminary to sexual intercourse, but as a normal everyday rubric of their common life. Such play is, in fact, so ordinary and accepted that sometimes we do not even notice it. This ordinary love play has the characteristics of the dance: it has a certain predictability, but also surprises and, of course, delight.

Every family, no matter what its particular situation, has its moments of humor. Life is funny, and people do laugh in spite of everything. Humor, too, is part of our playing.

Rahner asks the question: Did Christ ever laugh? I can't imagine that he didn't. He seems to be precisely the kind of man whom Rahner calls "grave-merry," a man who feels himself invincibly secure, but also a man of tragedy who sees through the masks of the game of life.[13] We know that Jesus wept. He wept over Lazarus and he wept over Jerusalem and who knows what else. I think he probably wept when he saw the poor widow put all she had into the temple treasury. If Rahner is right in his view that laughter and tears are close to each other, then a man who weeps must surely laugh. I think Jesus laughed at the sight of Zacchaeus in the tree, and I think Zacchaeus laughed with him. It was a funny sight. I would be surprised if Jesus didn't laugh with the woman at the well. Their dialogue has enough irony to occasion laughter. And there were dinners and parties and weddings attended by Jesus and his friends. These are not usually gloomy events. I think Jesus laughed a lot.

The Child Within

Psychology has been enriched in recent years by research into the stages of adult development. For a long time it had been assumed that adulthood meant that one was "finished," that development had reached its goal: one married, had children, and settled into expected and respected roles. Erik Erikson theorized differently, and gave us a foundation for a fresh look at adult maturation. Other pioneers, such as Robert Havighurst and Bernice Neugarten, investigated the tasks that adults undertake at various stages in life. Now it is understood that there is inner growth, change, and development of the whole person throughout the whole of existence.

This development is often expressed in terms of life passages. Evelyn and James Whitehead have studied these passages and reflected on them in terms of their religious meaning.[14] The mid-life passage, they suggest, may be most significant in allowing a person to reconnect with his or her inner child. The mid-life period is one of mature generativity, the time of handing on to the next generation the tasks of responsibility. The handing over is an act of trust because we know that what we bequeath is likely to be changed. Here, we let go and let others go forward. The Whiteheads believe that if we successfully negotiate this passage, that is, if we really hand over the reins in trust, we enter into new opportunities for mature childlikeness, the paradoxical ideal of maturity that Jesus gives us in the Gospel. They point out that the child is less defined by sexuality than is a young adult. Others note that the child can enjoy time alone, in touch with the inner world, with all its beauty and all its potential destructiveness.[15] Once we have released the reins of total control over job and family and success, and opened the door to others, a new door opens for us. A life of fantasy and imagination can lead us to explore. We can let our inner child out to play.

Playing and Working and Praying

Abraham Maslow was probably the first psychologist to note that adults who had successfully met and integrated a hierarchy of needs in their lives experienced their work as play. These people don't work in order to play, but, in a sense, their lives are play. The people whom Maslow studied, self-actualized people, had found an integrating principle in their lives. They were passionately committed to science or art or exploration or teaching or medicine. They were aware of a spiritual reality in the universe, although they were not necessarily associated with organized religion. They were keenly aware of the divine mystery, however. Their lives were given to their work, and they considered their work a gift.

There is a difference between compulsive work and work as play. The former is concerned with results and achievement and recognition; the latter is experienced as the outward manifestation of the inner life. The expression "one works to live" takes on new meaning in this context. Nonetheless, even when work is that which delights our heart and flows from the very core of our being, wisdom dictates a pause. The body needs rest and so does the soul. This rest is like the quiet experienced by the sparrow that has come home (Psalm 84), and like the trust expressed in Psalm 94: "I need only say 'I am slipping'; and your love, Yahweh, immediately supports me." It is possible with trust, to sing and to play in the depths of one's soul.

More Play

I have discovered that I do play after all. I laugh and cry. I feel renewed in my work. I dream, day and night. I like to sit with God. My husband and I play our particular and private games of love. I am more aware of each day now, and also more willing to let it go.

But there is more. I would like to play some nonverbal games. I have a fantasy in which I weave and crochet several hours a day. It is an abiding image, so maybe it really can be actualized. And I have a wish to be uninhibited bodily, maybe even to dance.

I hope eventually to love at least one other person with my whole self, with all my mind, all my body, all my emotions, all my spirit, all my strength. To do so requires learning and practice, and the unself-consciousness of the child. To do so I must heed that often heard parental directive, "Go out and play!" I think that those who do heed it will say with the blessed Saint Perpetua in heaven, "Thanks be to God! As I was merry in the flesh, now here I am merrier still."[16]

Chapter 7

STUDY

I still have many things to say to you, but they would be too much for you now. But when the Spirit of truth comes, he will lead you to the complete truth.

John 16:12–14

Learning is a gradual thing, a slow unfolding within each of us. We do not learn all things all at once. Instead, we move toward the truth, a little at a time, under the shadow of the Spirit.

Gradual learning happens in different ways. It is basic to educational systems, for instance. We progress through school, acquiring information, analyzing it and judging it. We call this study, and it is an essential part of the development of the human person in contemporary society. But there is another aspect to gradual learning, what Plato calls reminiscence. Like Christians, Plato believed that the human soul is immortal, and therefore the seeds of all knowledge are there. What remains is for a woman or a man to uncover that which has always been present within, to bring it forth, to educate oneself and others. This is also one of the basic insights of Zen. In Zen, there is the concept of true learning, which is an awakening to the *one self* that has the same source as all creation. In true learning, one experiences (and so knows) relationship and unity with all of life, and there flows from this an integration of the intellectual and the behavioral sides of the human person. The result is that we live what we know and we know how to live.[1]

Thomas Merton sees this true learning to be at the heart of the monastic vocation. "The monk does not come to the monastery to 'get' something which the ordinary Christian cannot have. On the contrary, he comes there in order to realize all that any good Christian already has. . . . He comes in order that he might see and understand that he already possesses everything."[2] The tough gentleness that characterizes both Zen and Merton's perception of monasticism is found in the stated intent of Saint Benedict:

> And so we are going to establish a school for the service of the Lord. In founding it we hope to introduce nothing harsh or burdensome. But if a certain strictness results from the dictates of equity for the amendment of vices or the preservation of charity, do not at once be dismayed and fly from the way of salvation, whose entrance cannot but be narrow. For as we advance in the religious life and in faith, our hearts expand and we run the way of God's commandments with unspeakable sweetness of love. [RB: prologue]

This expansion of the heart involves, I believe, the study of the human sciences as well as the true learning contained in the Christian Gospel. This is evident in the history of monasticism. During the collapse of the Roman Empire, for example, monastic writers found themselves called to preserve the human values of antiquity as well as to bear witness to the primary place of the search for God. Throughout history monks have engaged in the study of music and history, science and art, as well as theology and spiritual formation. Their contributions to the body of knowledge have been considerable. One venerable Benedictine is Bede, whom some regard as the father of English history.[3] His works include treatises on grammar, natural phenomena, the history of abbots, the ecclesiastical history of the English nation, and so on.

Not only learning but teaching as well has characterized

Benedictine life. Boys have been educated in Benedictine houses from the beginning, and the Rule contains some vivid disciplinary measures for maintaining order among the young (RB 30). At first boys who lived in the monasteries were destined to become monks. However, schools for boys who would live and work in the world eventually became attached to Benedictine monasteries, and education remains one of the principal works of the Benedictines today, for both men and women.

Like the monastery, the family home is both a place for searching after God and a vehicle for expanding human awareness and knowledge. It, too, is a school of study and true learning.

Study

It is usual to advise young people who are considering marriage to complete their education first. Generally speaking, this is good advice. It is sometimes coupled with the argument that financial security is also helpful for a successful marriage. This also contains some truth. The trouble comes when such advice takes on an absolute tone with the implication that not until life is in perfect order is there time for commitment. If, however, we look at family life and responsibility as a way of learning, then it becomes a pathway toward meeting the developmental tasks of young adults: establishing intimacy, building a home, having children. It is important to remember that education never ends. Formally, of course, it does end; but for men and women open to the world it goes on and on, as Plato suggests. As for financial security, that must surely be a relative evaluation. Who sets the standards for security? Where is the risk that always characterizes the call of God to us?

Oddly enough, our family has now seen two generations of married students. My husband and I were married when he was in graduate school. He finished his formal studies with the birth of our second child. In a sense, our family life began in the midst of study and financial insecurity. When our fourth and youngest child was three I returned to graduate school. I noticed a strength and clarity in this undertaking that was missing in my premarital studies. Now we see history repeating itself, in a way. One of our daughters, who had left college after one year, returned to full-time studies after her marriage, more secure and purposeful than she was before. What I see in both of these experiences is the psychological, spiritual, and emotional anchoring in marriage that can permit energy to be directed to something other than emotional needs. I have heard this confirmed by university professors who say that many of their most serious and dedicated students are married. As in the monastery, marriage and family can provide commitment, ritual, and community support to enable one to undertake the discipline required for serious study.

It would not be surprising to find that there are more married women than married men currently enrolled in institutions of higher education. Many women are finishing degrees that were put aside for marriage and children or for their husband's education. Some are starting down entirely different roads of study. In both cases, universities and other educational institutions are increasingly sensitive to the needs of women who are attempting to combine family and serious study.

There are many reasons why so many women are returning to school. Certainly the women's movement has been a catalyst in sharpening and defining new goals for women. Technology is also a factor; machines now do much of the housework, and time has been freed for women to make new choices. (The emerging field of women's studies provides information and analysis about the various aspects of this contemporary phenomenon.)[4]

While there are a number of common cultural and social forces involved in the continuing education of women, every woman's story has its own particularities.

Pat, a woman in her mid-forties, has been studying for most of her adult life. Her earliest recollections of vocation have to do with medicine and healing. It was natural, then, for her to choose nursing as a college major, as a preparation for medical school. When she learned that a nursing degree would not qualify her for admission to medical school, she chose to study sociology. Plans for medical school were put aside when she married immediately after college. For a while, Pat settled happily into full-time homemaking. Three children made this not only appropriate but enjoyable. When the children were all in school, Pat's energy, her intense interest in people, and her early desires to be involved in medicine pointed her once again toward nursing. She entered nursing school about the same time that she was "becoming a Christian in a real and decisive way." She finished her course of study, encouraged and helped by her husband, and subsequently began part-time hospital nursing three nights a week. The night shift was a reasonable arrangement, she says, since her husband could be at home with the children.

After four years in the hospital job, Pat and her husband separated. Concern about her children, and her own need to reevaluate her future convinced her to leave nursing. The coming apart that is often a stage of growth in Christian life happened in a traumatic way in Pat's case. Her Christian formation had taught her the value of community in times of stress, not only to cope with the stress but also to trust that God is in the coming apart. Consequently, her commitment to church intensified, and this, she believes, led her on yet another path of study: theology. She remembers a retreat she made around the time of decision: these were silent days in a secluded place of prayer. Out of the silence came the sure sense that she was being called to serve God in some form of direct ministry. As in the past, she searched for ways to prepare herself. All signs pointed to the seminary, where she presented herself to the dean, told her story, applied for admission, and was accepted. The four years of full-time study combined with part-time parish work were draining, but they were also years of true learning. She and her children learned through experience that equality and authority are parts of the same reality. The children believed in their mother's calling, and they knew they were needed in practical ways if she were to follow that call. When Pat received her divinity degree, the rejoicing was shared.

How do all these pieces of study and learning come together for Pat? She thinks that perhaps she may some day serve in a hospital as a chaplain. If this should come to be, she could bring to the sick, the frightened, and the brokenhearted a wealth of skills and wisdom developed out of attentive listening within, patient discipline without, and utter trust that God is present in all the unexpected events and people.

Children and Study

That parents and home are the primary educators of children is indisputable. But what does it really mean? Certainly it means that we indirectly teach our children by who we are. They know what is true about us and what is not. They know what we cherish and what we do not. It means, too, that parents can create an environment that helps both study and true learning. If we read books, frequent the library, explore ideas, are challenged and changed, and include our children in all of these experiences, we are educating them. Furthermore, we are providing structures for study within the home.

In the ancient world, skills were usually handed down from father to son. Apprenticeship to a master was conceived of as a father-son relationship. The monastic tradition reflects this in its stress on imitation as the primary means of learning. Parents have a range of skills that once identified can be taught to their children: they know a lot about how to make a home, how to maintain it and make it beautiful. Everything from carpentry to flower arranging can be important in the home education of children, and not only for the skill itself but also for the time shared between parent and child. And, as all teachers know, learning happens on both sides of the transaction.

Carla Needleman describes something of this parental self-discovery in her reflections on her pottery students:

> While we were working together I felt how different we were and how locked each was in her own attitudes, in her own space. I felt our lack of self-understanding with a certain degree of wonder. When and how did it happen that I became like this and not the way she is? Somehow she found her own quiet way of understanding what was needed and learned to center the clay, learned even to formulate the words to tell me what she found. The small pots she has made since are very light and lovely, carefully done, the shapes simple, classically fine. Perhaps after all, there had been an unseen exchange of understanding between us, a magical osmosis through the tough membrane separating us. I know only that I am happy for her success. I don't know and I probably will not be able to know if her experience with me and with the potter's wheel will affect her life outside the studio.[5]

There are parallels in the family. I help a child with his homework, and at first he seems determined not to understand. If I stay with that perception, I either leave him to his own devices and hope the teacher will straighten him out, or else I accuse him of being obstinate. Tears. If I step back a bit, in the Needleman manner, and marvel at the difference in us, maybe I can wait with him a little longer, until he finds *his* way into the work.

I decide to teach him to set the table—correctly. I can give him directions: the forks go here, the napkins there. Then I can leave, come back, correct his mistakes, or do it myself. Or, I can *be* with him, giving him my time, my precious time, as he learns about flowers and candles and knives and plates.

In both instances, I might ask, has my son learned more than mathematics or more than the art of table setting? Will my teaching affect his life outside the home? Maybe. Will it affect my life? Assuredly.

Young families of our generation and in our social milieu wrestled with the question of whether to have television in our homes. Some began married life and parenthood without television, as we did. I think it was football that finally brought television within our walls. However, when the television periodically broke down and money was not readily available we would be without television for several months. Once it was gone for a year. Everyone survived—and we even grew to enjoy its absence. But it returned, always for a good purpose: election night or an educational series, but mostly for football. Undoubtedly it's here to stay, but at least everyone knows it is a dispensable item.

Personally, I have serious doubts about television as a teaching or learning tool, despite the fact that I worked in educational television for several years. I do not believe that anything truly important can be learned without personal human interaction. True study, as well as true learning, requires opportunity for questioning, for waiting, for arguing. It requires time, which is so costly in television. And it requires human relationship.

This is not to say that nothing educational is available through television. Like museums, television can bring to us the treasures of history and science and art, linking our awareness to the giftedness of the past. But to discover the treasures within our own hearts, we need the evocative presence of community.

True Learning

Carla Needleman asks, What is the craft of being human? I answer that families are one way of finding out. They can be the studios for working on that craft, for whittling away the sharp edges of ego that keep us from learning the truth. Marriage and families are opportune arenas for learning what it means to be a man, what it means to be a woman, what it means to be a person. True learning about this can make a difference to the world.

That we each carry within us the sexual other is not so shocking any more. Carl Jung brought this to public attention, and now most of us realize with some conviction that each man carries within himself a feminine principle, the anima, and that each woman carries within herself a masculine principle, the animus. According to Jung, these inner men and women reside in the deepest parts of our psyches, bridging unconscious contents to the soul. Because they are hidden so deep within, the feminine and masculine components remain unknown. Unconsciously, however, we project the animus or anima contents onto others. For the most part, man has projected the anima onto woman and woman has projected the animus onto man. The result has been that woman has carried for man the living image of his own feminine soul, and man has carried for woman the living image of her own spirit.[6] This process of projection can serve as a mirror in which we may see reflected our own psychic contents. Unfortunately, getting to that point of realization may be quite painful. When we are projecting our inner contents onto another, we do not see the other as he or she really is, in the fullness and autonomy of personhood. In John Sanford's words, "the human reality of the individual who carries a projection for us is obscured by the projected image."[7] These projections are often full of sexual attraction.

In marriage, where the nearness of day-to-day living reveals the partners in all their humanity, projections often move to those outside of the marriage relationship. This may disturb the marriage, according to Sanford, but psychological understanding can illuminate what is really going on. Marriage, then, can be a path toward wholeness, allowing two people to "bump up against each other's areas of unconsciousness."[8] Wholeness comes when we allow the buried parts of our souls to emerge. If we are persevering men and women, willing to live through the painful experiences (the crucifixions), we can discover in and through the marriage relationship a kind of salvation that comes from being at peace with the animus or anima.

In Jungian terms, it is the anima, the feminine in both men

and women, which is the soul, the spark of divine energy. Some have thought that women are closer to this reality than men are, because the anima, the feminine principle, is familiar and not alarming. For men, however, the feminine, within or without, is more mysterious and perhaps frightening. Jung maintained that men would be helped through the difficult passage of integration with the anima by the presence and guidance of an understanding woman. A wife who has studied herself, her husband, and others, can be such a guide for the true learning that includes affirmation of the feminine in all persons. To be helpful she will often have to be silent and aware, letting her husband try to articulate the fearful mystery within, encouraging him to grow toward wholeness. Her role is perhaps like that of the Jesus of the Gospel.

On the other hand, a husband can help his wife by being supportive of her efforts to develop the objective side of her life, especially the development of her intellectual and creative side. Some understanding of the psychological inner figures can help men to realize why their wives cannot be totally wrapped up in the realm of family and husband. Men who are enablers of their wives' ventures become partners in their adventures. (Like the creative love of the Holy Spirit, perhaps?)

The Family: A Community for True Learning and Contemplation

Study and work (and play) are closely allied. We all study for our occupations and then work at them. Sometimes our work is consciously felt and experienced as the expression of the interior person. This is especially true of artists, scientists, and teachers. They are persons who experience their work as vocation, as life, even. How does family fit into such a life? Do spouse and children enhance one's life work? Does one's life work contribute to the true learning and spiritual growth of the family community? It can.

Frank Wright is a Washington, D.C., artist. He studied at

American University and in Europe. His work includes print-making and incredibly detailed oil paintings. After many years of being unknown, he has now achieved recognition.

He married at the beginning of his artistic career and his wife was the subject of many of his early paintings. In an interview in *The Washington Post,*[9] he spoke revealingly about the centrality of his marriage and family in the development of his work. He told how both partners in the marriage have worked, he as a teacher, his wife in government. He said, "I never sat back and painted while she worked. I couldn't have done that." He remembers 1966 as a year when two wonderful things happened: he began teaching at the Corcoran Gallery and his daughter, Suzanne, was born. It was then, he said, that the idea came to him to do an ongoing chronology of his family, "not to sell, but for my own delight." He began making more realistic, autobiographical paintings, with a special interest in time and changes. As he continued his work, he developed techniques of light and color. He also began full-time teaching at a university. About this period he says, "Since then it's been a steady stream of working, teaching, and watching my daughter grow."

But his life and artistic work have not been without crises. At one art show several years ago his new realistic paintings were not well received. This forced him to consider two questions. Why do I paint? What do I want to paint? His meditations led him to conclude, "Since I couldn't have commercial success, I decided from then on I'd do what I wanted. And in the process of doing what I wanted, I gained everything." And what was that? In addition to large historical paintings of downtown Washington, Frank Wright has focused on intimate scenes of his family: eating, lying in bed reading the funnies, listening to music, and just "generally enjoying a good contemplative life." And that is exactly what Frank Wright's paintings reveal, the contemplative dimension in the ordinary acts of family life. In his paintings one sees the grace of women setting the table, the light on an oriental rug, a child watering plants, the artist playing Beethoven while wife and child sit silently listening.

Not all of us have this gift for deeply personal work. We can, however, look at all that *is* given to us, each day, as coming from God, and gradually we can see more of what the Spirit would teach us. People are in our lives as revelations. True learning can be ours if we stop and ask questions like Wright's: "Why am I in this family? What do I want to learn here? What kind of life do I really want?" We must be prepared to give true and honest answers, or there will be little learning.

Even if our outside work is tedious and only a means of economic security, it can be transformed if we can see its connectedness to other parts of our lives. Uninteresting work sometimes allows people the economic freedom to develop their personal and spiritual gifts and to engage in ministry in the places of life that fall outside the boundaries of the job. Sometimes the uninteresting work itself can become a means for practicing ordinary contemplation, and the lessons learned at home can help with this. As Frank Wright's paintings show, the rhythms and rituals of a given day can be a means for sensing the transcendent. Waking and washing, eating and listening, looking and praying, reading, celebrating, planting, and talking can all develop a sense of presence that will remain with us wherever we are.

Home and family can be the school of Christian learning for ordinary people as surely as monastic life is teacher of the monk. At home, we can be emotionally strengthened and freed to study formally and informally all kinds of things, from geology to weaving, and helped to see the mysteries of the human condition. Within the community of marriage we can experience what it is to be whole men and whole women. The art of being present and attentive can be learned and practiced within the family as we undertake ordinary tasks. It is a way to learn extraordinary awareness.

Chapter 8

STABILITY

The place on which you stand is holy ground.
Exodus 3:5

"By the vow of stability the life of a monk is rooted in peace."[1]
I think most people long to be rooted in peace. What does that
mean for families, and how does it happen?

Studs Terkel interviewed a farmer in Tennessee, Herschel
Ligon, the fifth generation of his family to farm the same land.
Herschel has refused many offers to sell his land, concluding
that there is more to life than money. If he leaves, "What's
gonna be left for my children and grandchildren?" he asks. "If
my great-great-grandfather hadn't stayed, would I be here
now?"

Herschel Ligon speaks about his land with great feeling.

> There's nothin' better in the world than gettin' up
> before daylight and goin' and seein' the sun come up.
> Nothin' better than bein' in the field when the sun
> comes down, come in by the lights of the tractor every
> night.
> I intend to be buried up here in the family graveyard,
> out on top of the hill here. Everybody's up there but my
> great-great-great-grandfather and great-great-great-
> grandmother, which were buried in Williamson grave-
> yard. A child died and the snow was so deep, they
> couldn't get down to the Williamson graveyard, so they

buried the child on the hill over here. From then on, all
the Clays are buried in the family graveyard. I intend to
be put there, too. No question about it bein' continuity.
(Laughs)[2]

Clearly, the land and the place that holds the family, living
and dead, represent stability to Herschel Ligon. He stands on
the ground his ancestors farmed. He sees his descendants on
this ground and it is holy, soaked with their living and their
dying.

Not all families can so explicitly identify the place that gives
them stability. For many, stability can be found only in relationships.

This is seen in another Studs Terkel story, that of a woman
named Jessie de la Cruz, who grew up as a migrant worker. Her
story is about moving from place to place, with no farm or
ground to claim as her own. Jessie's memories are full of pain,
but also full of joy. She remembers Sundays, the day her grand-
father had off. He would wrap the children in blankets and put
them around a big wood-burning stove while he went to the
store. He came back with oranges and apples and other good
things to eat. About life in the labor camps she says:

> There were eight or nine of us. We had blankets that we
> rolled up during the day to give us a little place to walk
> around doing the housework. There was only one bed,
> which was my grandmother's. A cot. The rest of us slept
> on the floor. Before that, we used to live in tents,
> patched tents. Before we had a tent, we used to live
> under a tree. That was very hard.[3]

That was how Jessie de la Cruz grew up. But she grew up
strong. She married, had six children, worked in the labor
camps until Cesar Chavez formed a union. Then she became a
union organizer. Eventually her family stopped migrating and,
with some other families, they rented some land and farmed.
Her dream is for a lot of farm workers to be settled on their own

farms. Stability for Jessie has been found in her family, her fellow workers and the union. Justice and compassion and purpose flourished in these human relationships. Reading her story, you know she is formed in fidelity and perseverance. But, her story is like Herschel's in that she longs for land of her own; like Herschel, she is a farmer, in love with the land.

Saint Benedict and Stability

Stability is uniquely associated with monastic life. Unlike later religious orders in which members might be transferred from one place to another, the monk stays with the household he has joined. Saint Benedict wrote: "The workshop where we are to toil faithfully at all these tasks [i.e., the good works] is the enclosure of the monastery and stability in the community" (RB 4:78). These two aspects of stability—the place, that is, the monastic enclosure, and the community, the web of relationships within the place—are where salvation is to be found.

Benedict's concern that the monks live and perform the Work of God in one place arises in part due to the conditions of his particular historical situation. During the fifth and sixth centuries, monastic order and discipline were severely threatened by many wandering monks who were not accountable to any authority or attached to any community. Literature is filled with the adventures and misadventures of these religious nomads. The vow of stability, then, is generally viewed as one of Benedict's original contributions to monasticism. Thomas Merton looks upon this as a protection against natural human restlessness. He maintains that "by this vow the monk is reminded that he need not travel across the face of the earth to find God."[4] Monastic stability means that God is there on that holy ground, in that particular monastery, with that particular group of people with whom one chooses to praise God.

Merton cautions, however, against absolutizing stability. He warns against undue attachment to one's own monastery that can be a form of possessiveness. The place does have value, though, because it is a home; and Merton affirms that love of one's surroundings is good. At its core, however, stability lies in the monk's attachment to his monastic family. Merton writes, "The real secret of monastic stability is the total acceptance of God's plan by which the monk realizes himself to be inserted into the mystery of Christ *through this particular family and no other.*"5

Families and Stability

As the stories of Herschel Ligon and Jessie de la Cruz suggest, ordinary men and women instinctively know what Saint Benedict knew and what monks have discovered through the centuries. It is that people need a place and a community of people with whom to be in permanent and ongoing relationship in order to work out their salvation. All of us need a sense of belonging and security to help us face the unknown, both within and without. Trusting relationships usually allow this. A specific place, a home, gives us the location and the boundaries within which to work at the patient scraping away of ego-created illusions that block us from seeing ourselves, each other, and God.

The sacramental marriage vow is like the vow of stability. By it, we pledge ourselves to the search for God with *this* person, with *this* family that is forming here and now, although we may not be fully conscious of our pledge's implications for the divine search. No matter how conscious our intentions, life does not remain what it is on the wedding day. In a sense, the adult journey begins then, and the journey is one of many surprises.

Life Passages and Stability

Because of psychological research, we now know more about the needs and developmental tasks of the adult stage of life. When we marry, our need for intimacy is usually very pronounced and so is our need to establish a place of our own, a home. When these needs gain momentum it is likely that we will choose to marry, create a home, settle down somewhat, and eventually have a child. This moment of adult life is marked in all religious traditions by some kind of ritual, something that recognizes a passage from the world of dependence (or independence, if one is an older adult) to that of interdependence and commitment. No longer can one make decisions without affecting the people with whom we share life. This is not to say that in communities of single adults or in Christian households of faith persons remain unaffected by each other. In actuality, one of the effects of life in a family or a community or a monastery is to make us aware of our implication in each other's lives, not only where the immediate group is concerned, but ultimately in the lives of the whole human family. But the permanent nature of marriage and the creation of human life that follows this commitment usher one into the reality of adult responsibility very quickly. Other people depend on us for sustenance, for emotional, psychological, and physical nourishment. The passage into marriage impels us to some degree of other-centeredness. The passage into parenthood pulls us away even more from the demands of the ego. Together, these major life events constitute a critical moment in the developmental life of a person.

Marital intimacy and the fact of parenthood are watersheds in one's human and spiritual journey. Therese Benedek says of this dynamic moment:

> The fulfillment of love in marriage changes the psycho-dynamic interaction between the marital partners. Before fulfillment, before marriage, there was an exchange of ego ideals; in marriage, this becomes a relationship between two individuals who share the same reality. Common ambitions, desires, children, achievements of goals and/or their frustrations all may strengthen the identification between marital partners, be they positive or negative in their outcome. The depth of the identification is a consequence of the original intensity of the need which brought husband and

wife together, and it gives the relationship its exclusive significance, even after sexual passion has declined and the marriage appears to be a matter of convenience.[6]

For most of us it is our day-to-day living that occasions our adult human development as well as our growth in God. While the way is ordinary, it is not easy. Developmental passages always await us, challenging us to psychological and religious change. These are crisis times, and the presence of family not only supports us during the crises, family sometimes precipitates these critical moments. Living with others of different ages, we are forced to notice our internal and external changes. We grow older, our bodies change, our responsibilities change. We find ourselves launching young-adult children and caring for aging parents. Later we may find our resources of energy declining and our choices narrowed. These times of transition are not necessarily crises in the sense of marked stress and critical decisions. They may appear as teachable moments, as convergences within us that signal us to move forward, to change, to be converted again.[7]

Perseverance

Because transitions can make us feel unstable, they tend to pull us toward new experiences, to life on the outside. The pull may come in the form of a new relationship, church ministry, a new job, religious exercises—all potentially good in themselves. The issue is very subtle, precisely for this reason. New friendships, meaningful work, gifted ministry are signs of the Spirit, highlighting the teachable moments. These new experiences can, in the long run, be means of stabilizing family life. The difficulty arises when we slip into the illusion that God is more present in some other place, and so we leave our primary community in search of fulfillment, namely, God. The illusion can be so seductive that we forget the cautions addressed to those received into monastic life and those committing themselves to marriage. In both cases, persons are warned that difficulties and hardships await them. Yet they vow stability in one case and fidelity in the other. In both instances they consent to perseverance.

Monastic perseverance is more than merely staying in one place. It means continuing to live the life of the community, joining in the daily round of prayer and work, entering into the spirit of the monastery.

Family perseverance is similar. Physical presence alone does not constitute the fullness of fidelity. Emotional and spiritual presence, full and honest participation in the daily rounds of family ritual are necessary if one is truly to persevere. It is not enough merely to be looking on. To persevere in family life one must face the reality of all that is there, from caring for children to sickness to rejection and to death. All constitute life in community.

Part of the reality to be faced is that sometimes we fail to persevere, or sometimes another fails to persevere with us. The failure may be on the part of husband or wife, parent or child. Where lies the stability in such a situation?

Stability requires the recognition that most if not all families are less than ideal. In fact, imperfection is normal; and it is precisely there, in reality rather than in idealized fantasies, that God will be found. In practical terms it means that God is in the midst of unpaid bills and unwashed dishes, in the interaction between a difficult child and an impatient parent, in the strained silences that happen between husband and wife. God is there as all the sharp edges of our personalities are worn smooth in our encounters with one another. And God is there as defenses and false self-images are given up in the daily routines of living and working and praying together. God is there in our neuroses as well as in our health.

Saint Catherine of Genoa serves as a striking example of one whose personal family life could hardly be called happy. She was born in the mid-fifteenth century into a noble Ligurian family and was married at an early age to an aristocrat. Her life thereafter is described as one of loneliness, neglect, and neurotic melancholy.[8] She suffered from poor health, both physical and mental. Her husband not only systematically wasted his fortune, but he also had a mistress who eventually bore him a child. Catherine's reaction to all of this, at first, was to withdraw from everyone. After a while, at the urging of her family, she began once again to participate in the social life of Genoa but she was still plagued by depression.

Such a story is familiar in our own time, with men as well as women experiencing emotional abandonment. In Catherine's case, however, there seems to have been a direct intervention from God, marked by awareness of her past sins, deep sorrow, and an overwhelming sense of God's love. Baron von Hügel, whose definitive work, *The Mystical Element in Religion*, centers around Catherine of Genoa, says of this experience, "If the tests of reality in such things are their persistence and large and rich spiritual applicability and fruitfulness, then something profoundly real took place in the soul of that sad and weary woman."[9] The experience led to some radical changes in Catherine's life. Her prayer deepened and extended, while at the same time she led a very active life that included settling her husband's bankruptcy, dealing with his subsequent conversion, and beginning her ministry to the poor of Genoa. Later, Catherine and her husband, who had become a Franciscan tertiary, moved into a small house near the hospital where they tended vast numbers of the impoverished sick. This remained their principal ministry until their deaths. Records clearly indicate that Catherine forgave her husband everything, including his infidelity, and saw that some financial assistance was given to his former mistress and his child.

Friedrich von Hügel centers his masterful study on the personality of Catherine precisely because she represents so much of the ordinariness of Christian life, including extremes of the human condition. It was out of that condition that she entered into a most profound mystical relationship with God. Von Hügel describes her as "a person of intense and swiftly changing feelings, exaltations and depressions, [but also] one of a rich balanced doctrine and of a quite heroic objectivity and healthy spiritual utilization of all such intensities."[10]

She stands for us as one who encountered God in and through her less than perfect personal and family life, and who grew into the deepest mystical union with God. And lest we think that mystical union happens only in monasteries or hidden convents, we should note that Catherine remained in the world, in her marriage, in an active ministry of nursing, and eventually became director of a hospital, showing that it is possible to be "a saint among administrators," in the words of Serge Hughes.[11]

Catherine's way to God was through spiritual stability, perseverance in her marriage, commitment to her community of friends, and trust in her interior psychic experience and the direction in which it led her. The latter is, of course, the ultimate reckoning—for some it can mean leaving the community to which one has pledged stability.

Stability Away

What does a husband or wife do when confronted, for example, with abuse, rejection, or a decision on the part of the other to leave? Many in our time must face this reality. In this situation, separation and divorce must become the vehicle for encountering Christ. This happens in the crucifixion of alienation and loneliness.

A woman who is active in the North American Conference of Separated and Divorced Catholics described her own stages of grief and mourning when her marriage of twenty-five years collapsed. Both she and her husband had been involved in the community and in the Church. They had raised several children who were successfully launched in colleges and careers. Her husband had always traveled as a necessary part of his profession. His occasional absence from home was not unusual. What Ann began to notice, though, was that the quality of his being away and returning was different. When he came home, he was not really there. She says she can see now, with the perspective of distance, that she went through something akin to the stages of dying. First she denied to herself that her husband of so many years and so many shared experiences could possibly be having an affair with another woman. She bargained with God: let this pass and I will try harder. It did not pass, and eventually her husband told her he wanted a divorce and wanted to remarry. It was then that she felt anger, and later guilt. She could not help wondering what she had done to bring such a thing to pass. Even her children said she must have done *something* to drive their father away. The divorce took place, and she who had been so tied to the Church suddenly felt adrift. She had no moorings. Even though intellectually she knew there was no reason for the Church to reject her, she felt rejected. She is not clear about the source of the feeling, but she thinks some of it came from her own projections and some of it was genuinely present in the parish.

This all happened five years ago. With the help of a support group and compassionate pastoral ministry, her life is once again steady and purposeful. Her story recalls Psalm 22, which Jesus said upon the cross. It begins, "My God, my God, why hast thou forsaken me?/Why art thou so far from helping me, from the words of my groaning? O my God, I cry by day, but thou dost not answer;/and by night, but find no rest." The Psalm continues in a spirit of slender hope and trust, "Yet thou art holy . . . in thee our fathers trusted. . . ." It goes on, alternating between anguish and trust, at deeper and deeper levels, until a final anguished cry to God, "Save . . . my afflicted soul from the horns of the wild oxen." The rest of the Psalm is a song of resurrection, a reminder that Christ's resurrection began on the cross. One of the lines in this latter part of the Psalm is, "All the families of the nations shall worship before him."

Ann's story is contained in this Psalm, as are all our stories. Only the details differ. But what can be said of her and stability?

I see in her journey Merton's interpretation of stability as total acceptance of God's plan, by which one realizes that he or she is inserted into the mystery of Christ *through this particular family,* and in some particular families, the insertion into Christ may be through the trauma of divorce.

When families with young children go through divorce, stability can be experienced in the parental ties to the children. Single parents can grow in their self-giving through heightened awareness of their children's emotional and spiritual needs and by conscious attention to those needs, something that can be overlooked in a two-parent family where crisis hasn't prompted an examination of values. Stability is found in that kind of awareness and attention.

For the single parent, the wider circles of relationships also express stability. Friendship, other relatives, the Church—all convey to children and to oneself that God's stability is found in ever expanding boundaries of community and that the bonds of baptism are as real as the bonds of marriage or blood.

What of the person who must leave the family—a husband or wife or child who feels his or her salvation calls for this temporarily or permanently? There are those who love their families, who will provide for them and care for them, but who cannot live with them. The demands of family seem to destroy the fabric of their being. Some artists find this to be true, as do some religious personalities. The pull toward solitude is so intense that it can be ignored only at great peril. The monastic tradition again provides an analogue in allowing for the eremitical vocation. Who would want to be a hermit? Some people find it natural, like Matthew Kelty, for example, alone in New Guinea: "One does what one is called to. One does what one can. The basic call is to holiness, and holiness like Christianity, can be found anywhere, works anywhere. . . . I assert my right to be myself and to do as I see fit. Or more aptly, to do as God wants me to do."[12]

A person may enter marriage and establish a family not quite conscious of the deeper vocation that is slumbering within. He or she may sense such a call, be afraid of it and attempt to assuage the discomfort with marriage. So, too, with monks. Men like Kelty or Merton, vowed to their community and loving their community, could not deny the necessity of more complete solitude if they were to continue becoming. It is not unheard of in the annals of hagiography that women and men left homes and families and children to respond to what they perceived to be God's call. Saint Peter is one, Saint Francis of Assisi another.

Marie of the Incarnation, a seventeenth-century French Ursuline nun who became a missionary to Canada, is one who followed an inner call in a way that most people today would consider absolutely heartless. She entered the convent as a widow with an eleven-year-old son. The boy did what any boy who felt he was about to be deserted would do: he ran away. Later, when Marie had been in the convent for a while, he tried very hard to get her to return to him. He would go to the convent and ask if he could live with her. Once he brought a poem composed by one of his uncles describing the sorrows of an orphan.[13] He often went to the convent chapel, and to try to gain his mother's attention he would toss his coat and hat as a sign of his presence. His school friends shouted outside the convent windows demanding that Marie return to her son. All to no avail, of course. Marie remained in the Ursuline convent of Tours until she journeyed to the New World to begin a religious school for the Native Americans of Canada. How could she do this to her son, one might justly wonder? What kind of stability do her actions suggest? A letter from Quebec in 1641 written to her son, by then a member of a Benedictine community, explains her actions and her feelings:

> You have been abandoned by your mother and your kinsmen—has not this abandonment been advantageous to you? When I left you, you being not yet twelve years old, I did it only with great convulsions, which

were known solely to God. I had to obey his divine will which wished that things should happen thus. He promised me that he would take care of you, and then my heart grew strong enough to surmount what had delayed my entry into religion ten whole years.[14]

Jesus' own teachings about family leave little doubt that for one who follows his way everything but God is relative. Jesus says that those who leave houses or brother, father or mother or children or lands for his sake will receive a hundredfold (Matt. 20:29). Once, when he was preaching, his mother and relatives came asking to see him. He replied, "Who are my mother and my brothers?" And looking around him, he said, "Here are my mother and my brothers. Whoever does the will of God is my brother, and sister, and mother" (Mk. 3:32–34). The ordinary way of family life is not without unexpected turns, as God leads us down different and unimagined paths.

Stability and Place

Most of us in families would say that people are our stability, our own people who accompany us along the way. Yet a place to be and to live, a place to leave and return to, colors the quality of our relationships. Our places say much about us, the degree of formality or informality we desire, the kind of openness to others that we feel. Messages are everywhere. Our places speak our values, for we fill them with those things that give us life and joy and those things that connect us to our origins. What is absent from our places also reveals much to us and about us.

The room where I am working is small. An oversize desk takes up considerable space. Books, notes, a typewriter, and papers cover all the surfaces. When I stop working and look around, I feel overwhelmed by the disorder, but the energy is not available for ordering this small piece of my environment. The energy is all going inward, in the effort to order thoughts and feelings and words. When the book is finished there will be time and interest in outward arrangement. For now, the familiarity of it all holds me to my task. It is familiarity which frees all of us for exploration in other areas. At home, we know where things are, what we can rely on, what is predictable. In our own places we don't need to be constantly alert to danger, nor do we need to make hundreds of small decisions. Routines take over for us and allow us to rest and relax; they release us for work, service, and ministry.

Stability of place can be a gift, even if it is enforced stability. Illness fixed the writer Flannery O'Connor in one place, the family farm outside Milledgeville, Georgia, where she lived with her mother. Sally Fitzgerald in her introduction to *The Habit of Being* says of Flannery and her place:

> When she came home to Georgia for good, it was of course under the hard constraints of disseminated lupus erythematosus, a dangerous disease of metabolic origin . . . which exhausts the energies of its victims and necessitates an extremely careful and restricted life. But her return was for good, in more ways than one. She herself acknowledged this, describing it in one of her letters as not the end of all work she had thought it would be but only the beginning. Once she had accepted her destiny, she began to embrace it and it is clear from her correspondence that she cherished her life there and knew that she had been brought back exactly where she belonged and where her best work should be done.[15]

Flannery lived by routine, establishing living and working habits that would channel whatever strength she had into her writing. Her life was pared to essentials. Rooted in her place as she was, she looked into the heart of the life around her, her ducks and geese and peafowl, her friends and visitors, the richness of Southern people and customs, and then she crafted what she saw and heard and felt into her legacy of literature.

Limitations can offer us creative stability.

Symbols of Stability

Most families inherit or fashion for themselves symbols that carry the family's values and traditions. Religious symbols especially give families a sense of identity and, therefore, a sense of stability. Advent wreaths and Christmas trees, birthday candles and baptismal candles, Easter baskets and flowers and holy water, special food and special fasts all serve as bearers of religious tradition. They give us a sense of ourselves as a family but, more importantly, of belonging with other families in a common heritage. More important still, they remind us that the heritage stretches all the way to God.

I have known for many years that daily, dependable ritual calms both inner and outer chaos and confusion, but I have not recognized it as a mark of stability until now. I hope it will steady us for the uncertain future our planet faces. I have read stories of the Holocaust that describe Jewish families being taken from their homes on Fridays at sundown. In the back of a truck or in a cattle car, mothers lighted the candles and gathered the people for prayer. Headed toward certain destruction, they were a people who knew who they were and to whom they belonged. This knowledge had been cultivated week after week, generation after generation, at their family dinner tables. I wonder if our home rituals are strong enough to sustain us spiritually during the new holocaust that seems to be gaining momentum.

Stability is in the nature of family life, whether in a monastery, a city apartment, a farm, a suburban household—wherever. It is, however, an open reality; and it is expressed in different ways. What is common to all situations is simply the living of one's own story and the embracing of one's own reality, whether it be death or divorce, a husband or wife or parent or child with particular idiosyncracies, or the steady pace of everyday living. All is gift and grace, and it is proper and right that we should always and in all places give thanks and praise to God, who gives, sometimes, in mystifying ways.

Chapter 9

HOSPITALITY

> At the Oak of Mamre, while he was sitting by the entrance of the Tent during the hottest part of the day, he looked up, and there he saw three men standing near him. As soon as he saw them he ran from the entrance of the Tent to meet them. . . . "My lord," he said, "I beg you . . . kindly do not pass your servant by . . . let me fetch a little bread and you shall refresh yourselves before going further."
>
> *Genesis 18:1–5*

On that day Abraham entertained Yahweh, and Yahweh presented Abraham and Sarah with the improbable announcement that in their old age they would have a child. So improbable did it seem, that Sarah laughed at the thought of it. But Yahweh's word was true. Isaac was conceived and born, and so was the nation of Israel.

Generations later one of Abraham's descendants in a letter to the new Christian Church counseled those who followed the Christian way to extend hospitality to strangers, noting that in the past many had entertained angels unaware (Heb. 13:2).

In a sense, all the dynamics of Christian life are expressed in hospitality. Through the *intimacy* of marriage and family life we move toward a degree of self-acceptance that enables us to accept others, even strangers, into our homes and lives. As we learn about the relationship between *equality* and *authority*, we become clearer about the kind of life we invite others to share.

Solitude and *prayer* create space for others to enter, and quicken our imagination so we may receive them graciously. When others enter our homes, we will allow ourselves to *learn* from them, and they will find us, their hosts, ready to be engaged with them, drawing them out, entering their lives, too. Everything that goes into making a home flows out to those who enter.

In her most recent journal May Sarton records a fragment of a poem that she says is an attempt to suggest that maintaining a home is as much a gift to strangers who come into it as to the family inside.

> Though we dream of never having a wall against
> All that must flow and pass, and cannot be caught,
> An ever-welcoming self that is not fenced,
> Yet we are tethered still to another thought:
> The unsheltered cannot shelter, the exposed
> Exposes others; the wide open door
> Means nothing if it cannot be closed.
>
> Those who create real havens are not free.
> Hold fast, maintain, be rooted, dig deep wells;
> Whatever haven human love may be
> There is no freedom, without sheltering walls.
> And when we imagine wings that come and go
> What we see is a house, and a wide-open window.[1]

Receiving and Giving

We read in the Rule that all guests who present themselves are to be welcomed as Christ, for he himself would say, "I was a stranger and you welcomed me" (RB 53:1–2). Pilgrims, or those far from their own land, and the poor are singled out for special reverence, because in them more particularly is Christ received (RB 53:15). The Rule advocates a warm and open reception to guests and also provides practical directions for their accommodation, so that the life and work of the monastery will not be disturbed. (In an earlier monastic rule, even more directions were given concerning guests. One monastery, for example, allowed guests a week of leisure before being put to work in the garden, bakery, or kitchen.)

There is a delicate balance to be maintained between the ongoing rhythms, routines and rituals of the home and the change that occurs when guests are received. It is usual in our culture for guests to be invited in advance. So, in a sense, the household prepares for the event, whether it be a dinner party that lasts a few hours or house guests who remain for a week. Our reaching out to them and their response to us is an opportunity to share the stores of our gifts with others. It is a reminder that we are stewards only, that we do not own in any absolute sense the treasure of our lives.

When the children in a family are young, the parents must cleverly arrange and organize time so that they may have adult visits with their adult friends. And those with small children assume that dinner parties can never start before eight o'clock. As children grow and develop their own groups of friends, parental outreach to them can demonstrate that hospitality does not have rigid limits. It must have limits, as Saint Benedict knew, but the limits are there to preserve the good order of the home. This will mean that parents can define limits for their children's entertaining of their guests. It will also mean, however, that as children mature, parents will be sensitive to including their children in adult functions and will also be sensitive to their children's friends, inviting them to dinner or for dessert or to participate in some dimension of family life. Thus, in yet another way, children come to recognize the respect which their parents have for them and for their important outside relationships.

As our children and their friends have been growing up, we parents have made it a point to know each other. Some strong and lasting friendships have developed in this way; and during the always trying adolescent years, there was a feeling of a family network of adults who were ready to help *all* the young people. It is not unusual for our Catholic family to be invited to celebrate Passover with the family of our son's best friend. Nor is it unusual for us to include the parents and grandparents of some of our daughter's friends in our family celebrations. I think this kind of thing has built a foundation of confidence, not only for the parents, but for our "community children" as well.

Unexpected Guests

Through the years there have been others who have come through our door—all kinds of people, not only our cherished friends who are at the center of our common life, but also the pilgrims. They came as strangers but over the years some have become friends.

We live near the nation's capital, which attracts large numbers of foreign students. The Christian Family Movement at one time had an outreach program to them, which is how our family came to know Joseph, the son of a Coptic priest, who was a Christmas guest one year. A family of Bretons became lasting friends. Indonesian army officers in long-term training in the United States eased their homesickness for their own families by spending evenings with our children, telling us of their conversion to Catholicism and their efforts to establish Christian families. They left us with a bird of paradise, which in Indonesia is a symbol of immortality. And there was Benedict, an Ibo army officer from Nigeria, who went home to be killed. I shall never forget his brilliant smile, and whenever I think of Africa I pray for his rest and peace. There have been so many others who brought the richness of different cultures to us and stretched the walls of our house by their presence.

In the late 1960s and early seventies, Washington attracted not only students from abroad, but also Americans seeking to correct perceived injustice on the part of the government. The churches were at the center of these movements: the peace movement and the poor-people's campaign. The campaign created a huge tent city in the center of Washington, and the churches in sympathy with the campaign's goals tried, through a series of home meetings, to calm neighborhood anxiety about the presence of poor strangers in our midst. We held some meetings in our house. I had forgotten the intensity of feeling that the campaign generated among committed church people until I reread an old journal entry from that period:

> The people who believe the Church has no place in social action didn't come, except for one woman. The speaker for the campaign didn't come either. So there we were: white, suburban, middle-class people, of the concerned variety; Christian, for the most part, talking *to* each other rather than *with* each other. I felt compelled to divert the discussion toward the meaning of nonviolence for the Christian, using Pam's notes. There was no lag in the conversation, but to what end was it all directed? Last night, after everyone left I prayed, and this morning prayed for a long time. I feel sure God spoke to me personally in the unexpected events of last night. Odd. I expected God would speak, of course, but in a different way, the way of hostile or fearful white people confronted by some poor blacks from Selma, Alabama. Instead, God said, look at yourselves, what you must do in your own neighborhoods, within your own families, within your own person. To *me*, especially, God said, now you have a different relationship with people in your own neighborhood. This is true. I have never had deep bonds with neighbors in any place I've lived. *Friends* lived at a distance. I overlooked what and who were near at hand. Last night, through prayer and concern for the poor and common recognition of our hidden prejudices, something new happened between us.

The peace marches filled the city with young people who had no place to sleep, no place of warmth. They congregated in churches as they waited for homes to open to them before the next day's march. Four students from the University of Connecticut came to us. It was a cold fall night. We had hot tea and cocoa before they went to bed. At midnight the phone rang. Six more students who had driven all day from Wisconsin were in the nearby church with sleeping bags. Could they come to our home? My husband, not able to sleep anyway, collected them. He cooked breakfast the next morning while the soon-to-be marchers sang songs and I tried to explain all that was happening to our four curious young children. Some of the marchers were arrested that day. We do not think our guests were among them.

The unexpected guest who most affected our lives was an inmate of a state penitentiary. I will call him Kenny. One evening we received a call from a priest-social worker in a nearby city. Without any preliminaries he told us about a man he knew, an inmate who had been denied parole a number of times because he was without family or friends to help him find a place to live, a job, a support group—all that is necessary to "make it" on the outside. The priest told us that the man had been incarcerated, one way or another, since the age of nine. At that time he was thirty-nine. Everyone in the prison agreed that he was not pathological and should have a chance on the outside, but he needed help. Would we, could we help? Instinctively I knew that we could not even begin to think about this or pray about it alone. Kenny, as yet unseen and unknown, needed *community* care. At the time, we were members of an experimental parish, with liturgies consciously connecting worship and justice, and with a strong personal-support network. My husband and I went to Mass that day and prayed about the whole situation. By the end of the Mass, the next step seemed clear: we would go to the penitentiary to meet the man. And this we did, during the Christmas holidays. I will never forget my entrance into that prison. In display cases were the chains and irons and other instruments of restraint and control that had been used in previous times to secure the state's prisoners. I was suddenly and inexplicably overwhelmed by revulsion and terror. I told the chaplain and others who had arranged for the visit that I could not go through with it. My husband would have to go alone. The chaplain looked at me without judgment and said simply, "We went through a lot to gain admittance for you, a woman. We think this man's worth it. We hope you'll change your mind." I went in with my husband, the chaplain, and the guards. I was very frightened.

We met Kenny in the parole room where inmates' cases are heard. The first thing I noticed was that the chair in which the prisoner sat was nailed to the floor. Later I was told this was because the prisoners' anxiety is so high they would unknowingly be edging the chair forward toward the parole board's desk all during the inquiry.

We talked about us, our children, our efforts at family building. Kenny talked, too, about his family whom he hardly knew. He had been orphaned at an early age and his brothers and sisters scattered, forging their own lives somewhere. Kenny had been in a series of foster homes, and he had been classified as retarded. School ended for him in sixth grade. He ran away a lot, was declared delinquent, and was placed in security residences. In his mid-twenties, when he had no money and no prospects, he joined with another wanderer, bought a gun, held up a small business, escaped with about thirty dollars, and was arrested within the hour. He was tried, found guilty, sentenced, and jailed. But that was only the beginning of his prison life. He made many attempts to escape, some of them successful; but he was always caught. After every escape, "bad time" was added to his record. When we met Kenny he had been in state prison for about twelve years. He had been denied parole eight times because there was no one outside the prison to be his buffer.

What can I say about him? He was small, spontaneous like a child, anxious to prove his sincerity. We liked him. A quite irrational reaction linked us explicitly to Kenny and linked him to us. We liked him, that was all. Perhaps that fundamental stance toward him saw us through all the struggles regarding his parole. We visited a Gospel mission that was experienced in having prisoners paroled to their custody. The minister told us frankly, "Don't have him live with you; even apart from you it will be like adopting six children. He knows nothing about the outside; you'll have to teach him everything." The prospect was alarming. We sought help from our worshiping community. A small group formed, focused solely on helping Kenny. This small community became the extended family we so badly needed to help us with Kenny. We knew we were not alone. A temporary place for Kenny to live was found, an experimental religious community willing to house him for a while. He had no skills but he needed a job. A bottling company hired him, knowing his background and knowing there were likely to be human-relations problems. They were willing to give him a chance.

The week before Kenny was paroled the various law enforcement agencies that were involved brought him to visit the area, and our church group helped us give a welcoming luncheon. It was the strangest sight our neighborhood had ever seen. Squad cars lined the streets. Police officers, parole officers, state officials, members of a prayer community, and Kenny, a bit bewildered, all joined us for a noontime meal.

In the exhilaration we shared, none of us glimpsed the future problems that would occur. Kenny lost his first job, then another. We would step in, lend him money until he could get on his feet, and helped him look for other jobs. He wanted to make something of himself, so I, a professional educator, arranged for him to attend adult classes, which he didn't like because the other students did not speak English. It was then I realized how angry I was. The Gospel mission minister was right. I was relating to Kenny like a child who would not do what he was supposed to do. Somewhere in my psyche, I had planned a *program* for him and I thought if only he followed the program would he be all right.

In so many ways Kenny and I were worlds apart, not only educationally, but in tastes, interests, and style. While I had the community support group with me I could extend hospitality to Kenny. They were a protection, making me feel safe. Without them I felt at sea, afraid, I think, of a person whom I could understand but to whom I did not know how to be friend. I felt comfortable as his sponsor, his teacher—but friend? My husband, though, was able to be with him at some simpler, more direct level. He helped Kenny fill out unemployment forms; he met him for coffee, just to talk; he would drop in on him at his job or at his apartment.

Kenny lived in a neighborhood where crime was not uncommon. Eventually he was arrested again, this time for stealing. The parish support group worked with the court-appointed attorney, and Kenny received a light sentence. A year later he was released. The state gave him a suit, thirty dollars, and a bus ticket. He was back in our lives.

I had little energy for coping with Kenny, but my husband, as his friend, met his bus, found him a room, lent him some money and kept in touch. And then a most improbable thing happened. He began to long for his family, for blood kin whom he had not seen since he was nine. He was now in his early forties. One day he sat in the public library looking through telephone books for the city where he last saw his brothers and sisters. He found his name and next to it the name he remembered as his sister's. From a pay phone he called to this distant city and discovered that yes, indeed, the woman was his sister, Margaret, who had never married, who lived alone, and who wanted to see her brother. She flew to Washington. My husband took Kenny to the airport to meet her. Margaret heard about Kenny's long odyssey and, at the conclusion, asked him to come home with her. The whole thing seemed so improbable that those of us who knew Kenny laughed, just like Abraham's Sarah—except my husband, Kenny's friend. He told Kenny that family is a gift from God. Kenny accepted the gift, moved away, struggled to make a life with his sister. He's married now, the father of two children, and works as a laborer for the state. Occasionally

Kenny calls us from a phone booth to let us know how he is. Once he wrote a brief note to my husband. It said, "I'm OK. I'll never forget you."[2]

The more I reflected on Kenny the more I realized that what I was offering to him was not so much hospitality as techniques for fixing up his life. What my husband offered was friendship, simple reliable presence, a kind of stable hospitality. Out of this hospitable outreach, I think, God once again revealed the divine capacity for surprise.

Toward Others

The movement toward others outside the family becomes, I have found, a way of deepening our appreciation of God within us and within the family as well. The outward reach has the effect of strengthening a family; it is like the exercise of a muscle. With practice it becomes stronger. And there are many ways of exercising.

Intercessory prayer is one authentic outreach. Asking members of the family to pray for others not only makes them aware of segments of human need but asks for an investment of time and energy on behalf of those who are hurting or needy. Evelyn Underhill placed intercessory prayer at the center of Christian life:

> We cannot understand it, but perhaps we grasp its reality better if we keep in mind two facts. The first is, that all experience proves that we are not separate, ring-fenced spirits. We penetrate each other for good and evil, for the giving or taking of vitality, all the time. . . . The second fact is that the value and reality of our souls is at least as much social as individual. We do, and must, reinforce each other; make good each other's weakness. Each saint has something to give which adds to the glow of all saints: and only by self-loss in that one radiance can make his own life complete. Thus, intercession is the activity of a spirit which is a member

of this living society, this fabric of praying souls pene-
trated and irradiated by God-Spirit. All effective in-
tercession depends on the one hand on the keeping
alive of the soul's susceptibility to God, its religious
sensitiveness, by constant self-openings toward Him
. . . and on the other hand, in keeping keenly alert to
the needs of the world, through an untiring and in-
formed pity and sympathy.[3]

There are people and groups who take this so seriously that
they literally pray the newspapers each morning, a real and deep
reaching out to those unknown but nevertheless related persons across the globe.

Food is commonly associated with hospitality. People come to
us, or we go to them, to break bread together in the sacredness
of a home. Abraham urged Sarah to prepare food for the three
unexpected guests who appeared at the Oak of Mamre. The
deliverance of Israel from the hands of the Egyptians was and
is celebrated with a meal. Jesus' ministry is filled with occasions
of eating and drinking, and he continues to share his life with
us through bread and wine. Let us not forget the importance of
mere food, as May Sarton reminds us.[4] This means not only the
delight in enjoying the fruits of the earth, real though that is,
but the delights in bonding with people through a shared meal.
Meals are often occasions for our coming to know people we
might otherwise never have met. There are times, too, when the
gift of food consoles and conveys deep feelings. In our community, a new baby, a death, an illness, or a wedding means that
food will be brought to the home of those involved in these
special experiences. These meals, made by human hands and
blessed by God's love, are signs of human and divine collabora-
tion.

The choice of food can also be an opportunity to enhance
spiritual awareness, as is evident in every religious tradition. In
our day, more and more sensitized people are questioning the
way we unconsciously feed ourselves in affluent first-world

countries. As evidence mounts that what we grow and what we eat can affect not only our bodies and our spiritual selves but also the well-being of people in the developing world, Christians are exploring vegetarianism. This, too, echoes Saint Benedict, who directed his monastic family to abstain from eating *four-legged* animals (RB 39).

Letter writing is another form of hospitality, but it is apparently becoming quite rare. This is too bad because writing gives us freedom of expression to reveal feelings, thoughts, and hopes that are often left unsaid in conversations. Furthermore, letters have a lastingness. We may keep them forever. Like intercessory prayer, they are acts of loving concern because they are a tangible giving of time and energy to another. And like prayer, letters can ritualize life in a positive way, becoming dependable moments of contact between parents and children. They can be an outreach to the housebound or the institutionalized or toward those suffering loss. Letters are small links of commitment.

The Family and Social Responsibility

Marriage and the experience of family are deeply personal and intimate ways of being in life. Both society and the Church recognize, however, that marriage has a public character as well. For Christians, the sacramental character of their lives is marked by baptism, confirmation, the Eucharist, and, for many, in a special way by matrimony, a graced covenant, which has been called a "universal-concrete" love. Bishop J. Francis Stafford, chairman of the United States Catholic Conference's Family Life Commission, believes that the particularity of conjugal and familial love is a means by which the spouses aid each other and their children to live lives of universal love and social responsibility.[5] How this social responsibility is acted out will vary, but it is a dimension of hospitality that might be termed the outward mission. This dimension of outreach is as essential to the identity of the Christian family as prayer and worship.

Often, in fact, it is through the social outreach and mission dimension that the interior life of a person or a family group grows and deepens.

There are whole families, parents and children, who regularly serve breakfast once a month in a city mission for the poor and transient. The acting out of social responsibility need not be so dramatically visible. Boycotts, the decision to have only one car, the use of public transportation, growing a portion of one's own food, downward rather than upward mobility, are all signs that speak of social responsibility. The decision to be engaged in politics or volunteer community services is also an expression of social consciousness.

While some families may undertake an action together—passing out flyers or picketing—the social mission of the family can be carried out by one member on behalf of all. This is firmly rooted in Christian tradition, which uses the metaphor of the body and its members to describe the organic unity of life in the Church. And it must be remembered that the family *is* church, as Pope Paul VI said.

Saint Paul's explanation to the Corinthians about how the body works through members contributing their unique gifts for the good of all is particularly apt for the family. We see that it is not necessary for all members of a family group to be engaged in the same outward mission for the family to meet its social responsibility to the larger community. This becomes especially significant where growing children are concerned. Sometimes it is hard for parents to realize that their own social outreach may not take the form that is authentic for their children. Sometimes the appropriate role for children is simply to be themselves while their parents do what they must. On the other hand, parents of young children may need help in locating some appropriate social ministry for the entire family. More and more people find themselves in need of a supportive network and, fortunately, there are resources available.[6]

A doorway is a symbol of hospitality. People enter the intimacy of our homes through the doorway. It is there that we receive others. We, too, pass through the doorway, moving from the privacy of the home to the outside world, where we ally ourselves with the suffering and need that lie beyond our threshold, and where we ally ourselves, too, with the noble and beautiful works of humanity, and with the unknown. Abraham was sitting in his doorway when Yahweh appeared.

The experience of God in families happens in the comings and goings through our doorways. These daily pilgrimages are all so simple and ordinary that they can be missed. Children are blessed and go to school, husbands and wives go to their jobs, and all return at the end of the day to seek each other's face. Friends come for dinner; sick neighbors are visited. We go to church.

We pass through the doorway to be alone, to read, to pray in a secret place in secret silence. Finally, we send our children into the world to create their own homes, hopefully with ever wider doorways.

One day, our children's children's children will notice that all the world is home and all the strangers are family. I think on that day they will notice that God is indeed dwelling among the people. They will notice, our children's children's children, that God is wiping away every tear from every eye, and death shall be no more . . . (Rev. 21:4).

NOTES

Introduction

1. *Lumen Gentium* in *The Documents of Vatican II*, ed. Walter M. Abbott, S.J. (New York: Herder and Herder/Association Press, 1966), no. 40 (p. 67).

2. Marilynne Robinson, *Housekeeping* (New York: Farrar, Straus and Giroux, 1980), p. 185.

3. Pope Paul VI, *Evangelii Nuntiandi*, 1976, p. 51.

4. Evelyn Eaton Whitehead and James D. Whitehead, *Marrying Well: Possibilities in Christian Marriage Today* (New York: Doubleday, 1981), esp. chap. 13, "Intimacy—The Virtue at the Heart of Marriage."

Chapter 1 / Intimacy

1. John Dunne in *The Reasons of the Heart* (New York, Macmillan Press, 1978) develops the idea that the experience of love is finally the experience of seeing oneself reflected in the other's eyes. See also Brother Robert Englert's "Revelatory Rhythms in Prayer and Life" in *Spiritual Life* (Summer 1981).

2. Kenneth Russell, "Marriage and the Contemplative Life" in *Spiritual Life* 24, no. 7 (Spring 1978).

3. Ann Belford Ulanov, *Receiving Woman* (Philadelphia: Westminster Press, 1981), p. 79.

4. Pope John Paul II in a series of Wednesday audiences in 1979/80 spoke in depth about the meaning of full and total intimacy between man and woman. These addresses were published by *Osservatore Romano*, English edition, Vatican City. Cf. the issue of February 11, 1980.

5. Robb Forman Dew, *Dale Loves Sophie to Death* (New York: Farrar, Straus and Giroux, 1980), p. 200–1.

6. Cf. Andrew M. Greeley, *The Young Catholic Family: Religious Images and Marriage Fulfillment* (Chicago: Thomas More Press, 1980).

7. Archbishop Joseph Bernardin, "Marital Intimacy," an intervention given at the 1980 International Synod on the Family. Archbishop Bernardin's entire statement is available in *Origins*, vol. 10, no. 18.

8. Cf. *God and the Rhetoric of Sexuality* by Phyllis Trible (Philadelphia: Fortress Press, 1978) for a thorough examination of the feminine images of God in the Old Testament.

9. Bernard Lonergan's relevance for a theology of parenthood is to be found in Robert David Hughes, "Toward a Theology of Parenthood: The Place of Procreation among the Ends of Christian Marriage" (Ph.D. diss., St. Michael's College, University of Toronto, 1980).

10. Dr. Robert D. Hughes' thesis that children mirror their parents' unresolved emotional and spiritual conflicts appears in a paper prepared for a theological symposium held at the University of Notre Dame, as preparation for the 1980 International Synod on the Family.

11. Nancy Joyce wrote "Meditation on Watching" in 1975. John Joyce died June 1, 1978. The poem is published here, for the first time, with permission.

12. Aelred of Rievaulx, *Spiritual Friendship* (Kalamazoo, Mich.: Cistercian Publications, 1977), p. 93.

13. Paula Diehl, "Family Ministry in the Home: A Vehicle for Lay Involvement in Today's Church" in *Family Ministry: Resources for Implementation,* published with the permission of the USCC Department of Education.

14. Tilden Edwards, *Spiritual Friend* (New York: Paulist Press, 1980), p. 48.

15. *Ibid.,* p. 49.

16. Dorothy Day, *Meditations* (New York: Newman Press, 1970), p. 61.

Chapter 2 / Equality

1. David Parry, O.S.B., *The Households of God* (London: Darton, Longman and Todd, 1980), p. 23.

2. Cf. Jean Baker Miller, *Toward a New Psychology of Women* (Boston: Beacon Press, 1976), for a thorough explication of women's gifts.

3. Robert A. Johnson, *He: Understanding Masculine Psychology* (New York: Harper and Row, Perennial Library edition, 1977), p. 53.

4. *RB 1980: The Rule of St. Benedict in Latin and English with Notes,* ed. Timothy Fry, O.S.B. (Collegeville, Minn.: Liturgical Press, 1980), p. 368.

5. Dorothy Dinnerstein, *The Mermaid and the Minotaur* (New York: Harper and Row, 1976).

6. Cf. the documentation prepared and presented by the Pontifical Council for the Laity, at the United Nations meeting on women held in July, 1980, in Copenhagen. The delegates' interventions are available from the Documentation Service of the Pontifical Council for the Laity, Vatican City.

7. Cf. "The Changing Roles of Men and Women," a written intervention presented on behalf of the National Conference of Catholic Bishops at the 1980 International Synod on the Family. The text is available in *Origins,* vol. 10, no. 19.

8. Dolores Leckey, "The Spirituality of Marriage: A Pilgrimage of Sorts"; monograph prepared for the theological symposium held at the University of Notre Dame, as preparation for the 1980 International Synod on the Family. This monograph is available from The National Institute for the Family, Washington, D.C.

9. "The Changing Roles of Men and Women."

Chapter 3 / Authority
1. Hughes, "Toward a Theology of Parenthood," p. 193.

2. The Church of the Saviour, Washington, D.C., is an ecumenical church established explicitly on a theology of gifts. There are a number of books that tell the story of this unique experimentation in Christian community living. Elizabeth O'Connor is the author of many of these works. Also recommended for understanding the current development of gifts and ministries among all the people of God is *To Build and Be Church: Lay Ministry Resource Packet,* Office of Publishing Services, USCC, Washington, D.C.

3. David Parry, *Households of God,* p. 152.

4. Both of these sayings are found in *The Joyful Christian* by C. S. Lewis (New York: Macmillan, 1977), pp. 21–22.

Chapter 4 / Prayer
1. *Didache* 8, 3.

2. Parry, *Households of God,* p. 68.

3. Dr. Eugene Fisher, "Perspectives on the Family in Christian and Jewish Traditions," *SIDIC Jewish-Christian International Documentation* 14, no. 2 (1981), p. 9.

4. There are many materials available for parents and Christian community groups to help them enter into family liturgical prayer. I suggest that readers consult religious bookstores and publishers' lists.

5. The pastoral letter of Archbishop James S. Hickey, "The Sunday Liturgy in the Parish," discusses the liturgical roles of priests and all the baptized people. The complete text is available in *Origins*, USCC, Washington, D.C.

Chapter 5 / Solitude

1. *RB 1980*, p. 95.

2. *Ibid.*

3. Max Picard, *The World of Silence* (Chicago: Henry Regnery Co., 1952), p. 5.

4. Rollo May, *Man's Search for Himself* (New York: W. W. Norton, 1953), pp. 24–25.

5. Pope Paul VI, *Evangelii Nuntiandi*, 1976, p. 51.

6. Rainer Maria Rilke, *Letters to a Young Poet* (New York: W. W. Norton, 1954), p. 59.

7. John Dunne, *The Reasons of the Heart*, p. 21.

8. Dolores Leckey, *The Wind Is Rising: Prayer Ways for Active People* (Washington, D.C.: Quixote Center, 1978), p. 51.

9. May Sarton, *Recovering: A Journal* (New York: W. W. Norton, 1981), p. 207. All of May Sarton's work—novels, poetry, and journals—gives helpful insights into the experience, struggles, and joy of solitude.

10. Thomas Keating, O.C.S.O., "Contemplative Prayer in the Christian Tradition," *America* (April 8, 1978).

11. Cf., e.g., Kenneth Leech, *Soul Friend* (London: Sheldon Press, 1978).

12. Cf. M. Basil Pennington, O.C.S.O., for a complete treatment of the practice of centering prayer. His book, *Daily We Touch Him* (New York: Doubleday, 1977), is most helpful.

13. *Lectio divina* is a form of prayer that has been attributed to Saint Benedict, who popularized it and refined its use. It involves reading, meditation, and active prayer: After a period of quiet, one begins to read a sacred text, until a word or phrase attracts the attention. One then meditates on the word, dwelling on it, living for a little while with it. This is followed by direct prayer. For a short but thorough explanation of *lectio divina* see "The 'Benedictine' Method" in *Sadhana: A Way to God: Christian Exercises in Eastern Form* available from The Institute of Jesuit Sources; X. Diaz del Rio, S.J., publisher, Gujarat Sahitya Prakash, Amand, Gujarat, India.

14. A. M. Allchin, *The World Is a Wedding* (New York: Oxford University Press, 1978), p. 26.

15. Chaim Potok, *The Chosen* (Greenwich, Conn.: Fawcett Publications, 1967), p. 265.

Chapter 6 / Play

1. Hugo Rahner, *Man at Play* (New York: Herder and Herder, 1967).
2. Hugo Rahner regards this as one of Plato's important insights.
3. Augustine, *De Musica*, II, 14 (*PL* 32, 116 A).
4. Jerome, *Commentarii in Zachariam*, II 8 (PL 25, 1465B f.).
5. Rahner, *Man at Play*, p. 66.
6. *The Revelations of Mechtild of Magdeburg* (1210–1297); cited in Rahner, *Man at Play*, p. 55.
7. Teresa of Lisieux, *Autobiography of a Saint*, trans. Ronald Knox (London, 1958), p. 171.
8. Rahner, *Man at Play*, p. 76.
9. Gregory of Nyssa, *Homiliae in Ecclesiasten*, VI, 4 (*PG* 44, 709CD).
10. Rahner, *Man at Play*, p. 60.
11. The proceedings of this conference are now being prepared by the NCCB Secretariat for the Laity and the USCC Department of Publishing Services. The proceedings are entitled *Tree of Hope: A Consultation on American Spirituality.*
Both Matthew Fox, O.P., and Louis Savary have a considerable body of work that readers may wish to consult.
12. Walker Percy, *The Second Coming* (New York: Farrar, Straus and Giroux, 1980).
13. Rahner, *Man at Play*, p. 27.
14. Evelyn Eaton Whitehead and James D. Whitehead, *Christian Life Patterns* (New York: Doubleday, 1979).
15. Cf. Matthew Kelty on the fruits of solitude in *Flute Solo* (New York: Image Books, 1980).
16. "Passio SS. Felicitatis et Perpetuae," 12; cited in Rahner, *Man at Play*, p. 61.

Chapter 7 / Study

1. A full explanation of the meaning of *true learning* in the process of Zen training can be found in *Zen and the Bible*, by J. K. Kadowaki, S.J., trans. Joan Rieck (London: Routledge and Kegan Paul, 1980).
2. Thomas Merton, *The Monastic Journey*, ed. Patrick Hart (Kansas City: Sheed, Andrew, McNeel, 1977), p. 48.
3. *Encyclopedia Britannica*, 11th ed., vol. 3.
4. *Signs: A Journal of Women in Culture and Society*, which is published quarterly by the University of Chicago Press, is a resource for current

psychological, anthropological, and sociological research relevant to women.

5. Carla Needleman, *The Work of Craft* (New York: Knopf, 1979), p. 129.

6. John Sanford, *The Invisible Partners* (New York: Paulist Press, 1980), p. 10.

7. Ibid., p. 13.

8. Ibid., p. 81.

9. "Discovered," *The Washington Post Magazine* (June 21, 1981).

Chapter 8 / Stability

1. Thomas Merton, *The Monastic Journey*, p. 67.

2. Studs Terkel, *American Dreams: Lost and Found* (New York: Pantheon Books, 1980), pp. 148–51.

3. Ibid., p. 153.

4. Merton, *The Monastic Journey*, p. 67.

5. Ibid., p. 68.

6. James Anthony and Therese Benedek, eds., *Parenthood: Its Psychology and Psychopathology* (Boston: Little, Brown, 1970), p. 114.

7. For a thorough discussion of the possibilities for religious growth in developmental life, cf. Evelyn Eaton Whitehead and James D. Whitehead, *Christian Life Patterns* (Garden City, N.Y.: Doubleday, 1979).

8. Catherine of Genoa, *Purgation and Purgatory: The Spiritual Dialogue*, trans. Serge Hughes (New York: Paulist Press, 1979).

9. Friedrich von Hügel, *The Mystical Element in Religion* (London: James Clarke and Co., 1961), vol. 2, p. 29.

10. Ibid, p. 119.

11. "Notes on the Translation," p. 67 of Catherine of Genoa, *Purgation and Purgatory*.

12. Matthew Kelty, *Flute Solo*, pp. 66–7.

13. *Word from New France: The Selected Letters of Marie de l'Incarnation*, trans. and ed. Joyce Marslowe (Toronto: Oxford University Press, 1967), p. 8.

14. Ibid., p. 91.

15. Flannery O'Connor, *The Habit of Being*, ed. Sally Fitzgerald (New York: Farrar, Straus and Giroux, 1979), p. xv.

Chapter 9 / Hospitality

1. May Sarton, "Of Havens" in *Recovering: A Journal* (New York: W. W. Norton, 1980), p. 165. These lines from the poem are reprinted with permission.

2. The story of Kenny first appeared in the 1981–82 *Know Your Faith* series, published by the National Catholic News Service. It is reprinted with permission.

3. Evelyn Underhill, *The Evelyn Underhill Reader*, p. 95.

4. May Sarton, *Recovering*, p. 191.

5. Bishop J. Francis Stafford, "The Social Mission of the Family," a written intervention submitted to the 1980 International Synod of Bishops. Available in *Origins*, USCC, Washington, D.C.

6. For reliable information readers may want to contact the newly formed National Parenting for Peace and Justice Network, which is an effort to promote the integration of family life and social ministry. It is located in St. Louis, Mo.

Also, consult *Parenting for Peace and Justice*, by Kathleen and James McGuinness (New York: Orbis Books, 1981).

INDEX

potential, 3; marginal, 4; and
spirituality, 5; and intimacy, 33;
and Gospel authority, 59; and
common prayer, 66, 67, 68, 69;
and solitude, 83, 84, 85, 86; and
humor, 101; study and
contemplation, 116; and social
responsibility, 47, 143; family
ministry, 5
Feminists, 72, 89
Focolare, 72
Fredgren, Kathryn, 98, 99
Friedan, Betty, 41
Friendship, spiritual, 13, 25; in
marriage, 13, 26, 29; outside
marriage, 30; within the family,
27
Freud, Sigmund, 41

Genesis, garden of, 10, 19, 46, 47
Gifts of women, 39; of men, 40; in
the monastic community, 59;
related to authority, 56, 57;
personal giftedness, 77
God, as Mystery, 3; revelation of,
10; as Divine Presence, 11; in
Jesus, 11; as father and mother,
20; and contemplation, 22; God's
will and equality, 47; and play,
103, 104; in family life, 145

Havighurst, Robert, 102
Holiness, a universal call, 1
Hospitality, 8; and prayer, 75, 133,
141; and intimacy, 132; and
equality, 132; and authority, 132;
in the Rule of Benedict, 133;
toward children, 134; limits of,
134; toward strangers, 135; and
food, 142; and correspondence,
143
Hügel, (Baron) Friedrich von, 124
Humility, x, 61

Ignatius of Loyola, 78
Intimacy, 8; in Jesus' life, 12; in
early Christian communities, 12;
in desert Christianity, 13; and
friendship, 13; as sexual

presence, 14, 15, 16; of marriage,
17, 18; as self-discovery, 17;
cycles of, 18; parent-child, 20;
and prayer, 74; marital, 121; and
hospitality, 132

Jerome, 96
Jesus and intimacy, 12; Jesus
prayer, 89; teaching about family
life, 129
John of the Cross, 89
Johnson, Robert, 38
Journal keeping, 90
Journey and self-disclosure, 12
Jung, Carl, 41, 91, 113

Keating, Thomas, 88
Kelty, Matthew, 127, 128

Lectio divina, 90; 149 note 13
Liturgical seasons, 67
Lonergan, Bernard, 21

Marie of the Incarnation, 128
Marriage, preparation and
enrichment, 5; and intimacy, 14,
15, 16, 17, 18; and the Mystical
Body, 34; interfaith, 48; married
students, 107; and true learning,
112; marital play, 100; vow, 120
Marriage Encounter, 20
Maslow, Abraham, 102
Mechthild of Magdeburg, 96
Meditation and the rosary, 73, 88
Men, new choices, 39, 40, 41
Merton, Thomas, 106, 119, 120
Mid-life, 73, 102
Miller, Dr. Jean Baker, 38
Ministry, family, 5; within marriage,
17; family social mission, 143,
144
Monasticism, 6; and lay life, 7; and
intimacy, 13; and work, 41, 44;
and authority, 50, 59; and the
work of God, 63; and silence, 76,
90, 94; and learning, 106, 107;
and stability, 119, 123, 127; and
hospitality, 133
Montessori, Maria, 95